A NEW ZEAL
CYCLE TOURING

PEDALL
PARADISE

SOUTH ISLAND

NIGEL RUSHTON

Paradise Press
Christchurch
New Zealand

First published: October 1995
Second edition: September 2001
Third edition: September 2007

ISBN: 978-0-473-12604-9

I would like to say a special thank you to all the people who have helped in one way or another, voluntary and involuntarily!
Especially Eric & Aidy Foley, Yumi Sako

Also a thank you to:
NIWA for windflow characteristics

CONTENTS: SOUTH ISLAND

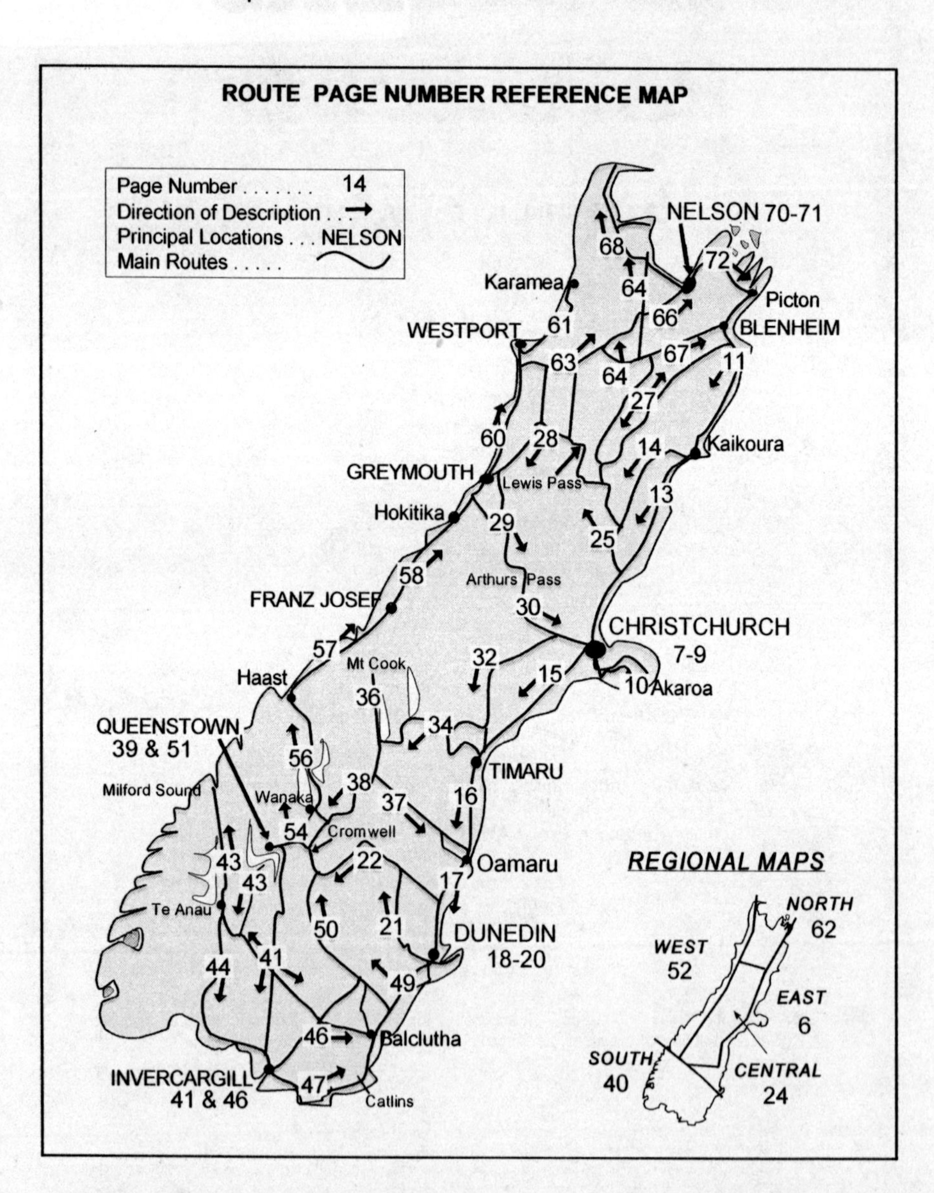

INTRODUCTION

ABOUT THIS GUIDE The purpose of this book is to provide a concise, practical and (hopefully) easy to follow guide for cycle tourers of New Zealand's South Island. The intention is to inform the users while still leaving something for them to discover.

NEW: In this edition the introduction has been reduced by one page to allow for more route information. Instead an expanded introduction is available on www.paradise-press.co.nz website.

Otherwise that is it, apart from minor cosmetic tweaking and removal of the author's genuine fingerprints on the back cover.

REGIONS: There are five regions as follows:

EAST between Picton, through Christchurch to Dunedin includes Banks & Otago Peninsulas.

CENTRAL Covers the central high country routes going over Lewis, Arthur's, Burkes and Lindis Passes, includes Mt Cook & Waitaki Valley.

SOUTH of a line from Queenstown to Dunedin.

WEST between Queenstown and Westport including up to Karamea.

NORTH of a line from Westport to Blenheim.

MAPS: Of the area covered are on the first page of each region. It includes routes, highways and some localities. Coastlines have been included in this edition as the author's computing ability is impoving.... and I'm getting better!!

SECTIONS: Each region is divided into sections and contain the following:

ROUTE: The routes described are usually main highways, presumes them to be sealed and says so if they're not. When an ALTERNATIVE, SIDE TRIP or LINK ROAD to/from the main route is available, there is a brief mention here with a more detailed account later. Major OPTIONS have their own sub-section. Influencing where a reader stops for the night is not intended.

In most cases routes are in their logical regions, hopefully! The obvious exception is Dunedin Ranfurly - Queenstown in East. This is to help the "flow" from one area of interest to another.

PROFILE: This is the side view of the route and is intended as a rough guide to the terrain. Distances in kilometres, elevation in metres. The steepness is exaggerated due to the distances covered, don't be put off! Only a selection of localities are shown, with a few places in between being indicated by a letter, which corresponds with one in Services.

SERVICES: Indicate what to expect in a location in terms of information, food, accommodation, cycle shop and sometimes transport. Most providers are open 7 days. The following brief definitions are for those new to NZ.

FOOD: 1 DAIRY: Is the smallest of food outlets. Usually found in suburbs or small locations. These outlets are similar to a corner shop or delicatessen. Sometimes they sell takeaways or other cooked food. This is the place to try the famous New Zealand ice cream. Yum!

2 STORE:is between a dairy and supermarket. Often linked to a grocery discount chain like Four Square or Pricecutter. Sometimes closed Saturday afternoon and/or Sunday.

3 SUPERMARKETS: Like others worldwide, even their names may be the same as elsewhere. Usually the cheapest place to buy food, but only found in larger population centres.

4 TAKEAWAYS: Sell food to be taken away such as those great cycling comestibles; fish and chips. It is not recommended to sit inside and eat without permission!

5 TEAROOMS: these days are often called coffee shops/cafés. A place to sit for lunch. Pots of tea are often good value. Ice cream and takeaways are usually available. Small rural one person operations may close on a weekday.

6 RESTAURANT: Same as anywhere in the world, the most expensive of all food outlets.

7 PUB: Public house or tavern; licensed premises where alcoholic beverages are sold. These are sometimes combined with a restaurant and/or accommodation.

ACCOMMODATION: 1. CAMPING: there are three categories as follows:

1a DoC CAMPING: Run by Department of Conservation. Often located in scenic reserves or national parks. Those adjacent to highways also make good rest stops. Basic facilities usually prevail such as long drop toilets, picnic tables and water. Most are "self registration" where users deposit fees in an honesty box.

1b DOMAIN CAMPING: Local council operated and located on public land (Domain). Those with basic facilities have a small charge or donation. Some are not advertised and only found by asking locals. Those similar to regular motor camps are listed as such.

1c MOTOR CAMPS: Or holiday parks.These are usually the most expensive camping. Facilities vary but communal kitchens and bathrooms are standard. Guests use their own bedding and cooking utensils but sometimes these can be hired. Many have cabins; often small simple huts containing beds. Considered the best places to meet Kiwis. A minimum two person charge may apply, even for solo cyclists. Obviously such situations should to be questioned.

2 HOSTELS: Provide inexpensive communal accommodation. Dormitories, common-rooms, bathrooms and equipped kitchens are standard. Guests bring their own sleeping bag but often linen can be hired. They're useful for up-to-date information. Some hostels allow camping. Some small hostels close in the off-season. There are two basic types of hostel:

2a BACKPACKER (or bkpr). Standards vary but BBH hostels are normally better than VIP. BBH has their annual BPP% customer satisfaction survey to help with where to stay.

2b YHA run by Youth Hostels Association, membership card required. Standards fairly uniform but usually more expensive than backpacker hostels. Note: All known camping grounds & hostels are listed.

3 MOTEL: Are self contained units and often includes an equipped kitchen.

4 HOTEL: Is often a pub with accommodation attached, sometimes a modern motor lodge.

Note: Some hotels may be closed on Sunday, particularly in country areas.

5 B & B: A guest house, farmstay or homestay. Usually small intimate places providing bed & breakfast, sometimes with 5 beds or less. These are not normally listed in this guide. Local lists are available at visitor information centres.

6 LODGE: This is a difficult one. This term is used by every level of accommodation. Often a wide selection is available in the same complex.

7 WWOOF: Willing Workers On Organic Farms. A work exchange scheme usually more suited to cyclists on extended tours and those interested in growing food the healthy way. Not listed here.

BICYCLE SHOP: The name and address of all known shops are listed on page 74, except in the big cities, where a selection is made. If possible check addresses for current listings, some may have changed. In places with no bicycle shops the mechanic at the local auto repair centre (garage) may be able to help.

TRANSPORT: Information on this is limited. "Bus" refers to the large 40 seater type, these are generally more reliable, comfortable and expensive than shuttles. Also "Shuttles" are often faster and more frequent than the larger buses.

Most buses and shutttles will take bikes, usually for a fixed fee regardless of distance travelled, but subject to available space. Bikes sometimes go separately from their owners. Some buses may also charge to take bike trailers.

GRADIENTS:This attempts to describe what sort of terrain to expect. Flat, undulating, rolling and steep are the basic variants. "Quite" or "fairly steep" is less steep than "steep" and "very steep". "Mostly flat" means at most a few minor rises and falls. "Undulates or rolls uphill" means the climb can vary with some short descents.

"Variable steep" means expect the gradient to vary and I have no idea what “gradual up or down” means! Confused? So am I!!

Gradients are probably the hardest part of the guide to get right. Wind, personal fitness and the bike’s load are important factors when assessing the degree of difficulty. I have presumed the reader is reasonably fit. When battling a headwind it is common to think you’re going uphill only to find it's an optical and cyclogical delusion! Not all hills are listed, sorry.

ATTRACTIONS: Include popular or unusual sights or activities an area has to offer, like swim with dolphins, tramping, sea kayaking and sheep-spotting. Boring activities such as golf, tennis etc are usually omitted. Fishing is possible almost anywhere there is water although it is not always mentioned. A valid licence is required.

OPTIONS: Are an **ALTERNATIVE** route, **SIDE TRIP** up a no exit or **LINK ROAD** to another major highway that may be worth considering, subject to the reader's preference and available time. Major options have their own sub-section, minor ones are listed under Options.

STREET MAPS & DIRECTIONS: and arterial route maps are only in Christchurch, Dunedin and Nelson sections. They provide information for getting into and out of the cities and replace Route. The easiest routes are described and take no account of how busy they are. Cycling on motorways is prohibited on all South Island motorways.

MISCELLANEOUS: **WEATHER:** This is the third most important thing in the entire Universe, after Pedallers' Paradise and a bike. NZ has a predominantly maritime climate and obviously it can only be described in general terms. Like weather everywhere it is largely unpredictable, which renders the next paragraph a waste of time.

Anyway, temperate climate predominates. The west has the most rainfall, Fiordland has recorded up to 8 metres! The Central high country tends to be the driest but is sometimes plagued by strong north westerly winds that can blow intermittently for weeks. Northern parts record the most sunshine and doesn't usually suffer the extremes of other areas. Eastern regions can be affected by cold southerly fronts coming up from Antartica.

Spring and autumn are generally said to be the best times to tour in terms of lower temperatures, smaller crowds and variety of hues. Unfortunately these seasons are susceptible to long periods of unsettled and windy weather, especially after the equinox. Mid summer can be very hot and humid. February and March are reputedly the best months for long settled spells. In other words "good luck"!

Winter cycle touring is possible for the well equipped but remember, wet gear takes longer to dry. It is rare even for alpine pass highways to close for more than a few days due to snow.

WIND FLOW CHARACTERISTICS

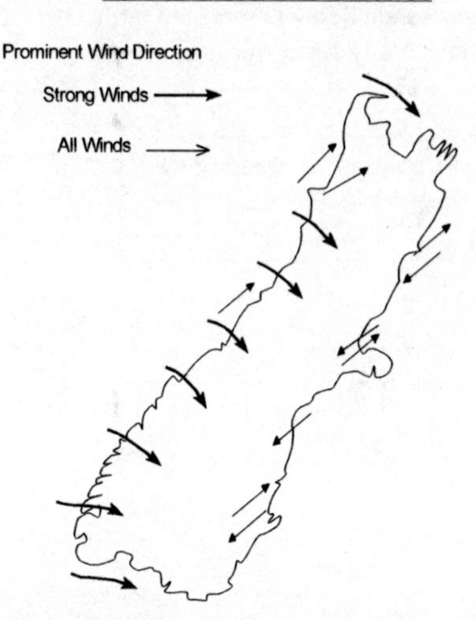

Weather forecasts are usually quite accurate but often get the days wrong! Those who carry a radio can hear a 5 day long-range forecast at 12:30pm everyday on National Radio. This non-commercial station is accessible from most of NZ but reception in some remote areas is poor. A bonus for foreign types is it provides the best national and international news coverage!!

MAPS: This guide can be used independently by those familiar with NZ but an additional map is recommended. Several organisations such as motor camps produce general give-away maps. The Automobile Association has excellent District Maps series that are free to members.

Otherwise several companies produce a variety of maps and road atlas'. Try KiwiMaps or Wise's 2 maps per island series. Both are 500,000:1 and quite reasonably priced. Another option is to use a road atlas, of which all the above companies produce them. Topomaps produce a variety of scales but are comparatively quite expensive.

OTHER: As stated earlier an expanded introduction including photographs can now be found on www.paradise-press.co.nz website.

EAST

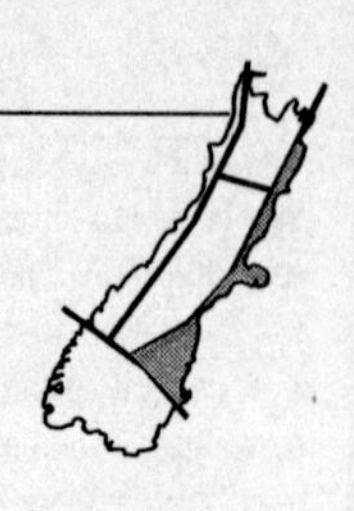

HIGHLIGHTS (not in any order of preference)

Christchurch City & Port Hills
Dunedin & Otago Peninsula
Whales & dolphins at Kaikoura
Marlborough Sounds Maritime Park
Penguins & Historic Precinct at Oamaru
North Canterbury coastal scenery
North Otago coastal scenery
Akaroa & Banks Peninsula
Otago Central Rail Trail &
Taieri Gorge Railway

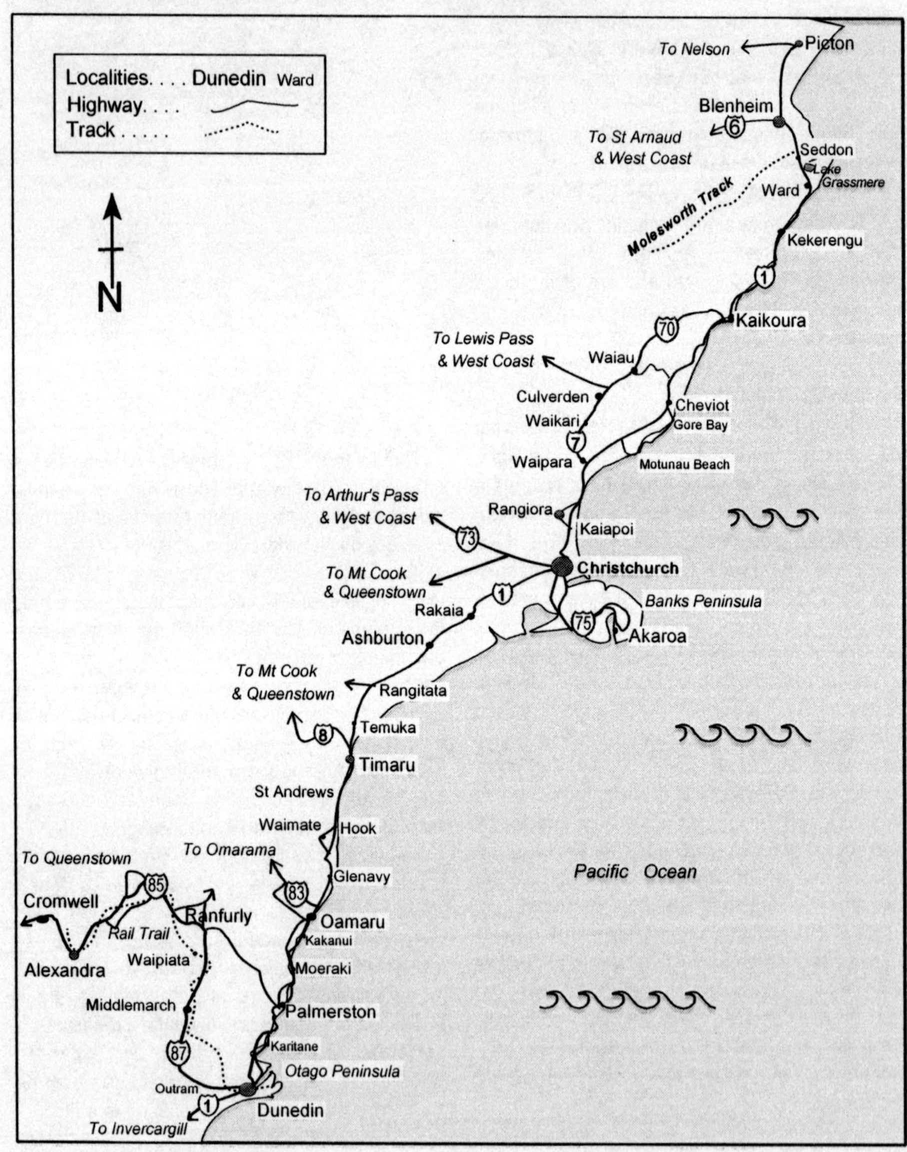

1 CHRISTCHURCH.

SERVICES: **CHRISTCHURCH:** Altitude 20m, population: 380,000.
i: 1) Old Post Office, Cathedral Square ☎379-9629. 2) DoC, 133 Victoria St ☎379-9758.
3) Domestic and International Terminals, Chch Airport. Food: Many of all outlets.
Accommodation: 9 motor camp; hostel (20 bkpr, 2 YHA); multitudes of motels and hotels.
Transport: Train to/from Picton & Greymouth. Bus & shuttles to/from just about everywhere on the South Island. Bicycle shops: See Apendix (page 74).

ATTRACTIONS: Christchurch is the South Island's biggest city. Often said to be the most English of NZ's cities, it has plenty of parks & gardens to justify calling itself the "Garden City". Cathedral Square is the heart of the city and comes complete with a cathedral but the Wizard has now retired.

Other attractions include the popular Botanic Gardens, Canterbury Museum, Art Centre and nearby shiny new Art Gallery. All conveniently close to each other, including the adjcent Hagley Park, one of the world's biggest inner city open space. New Brighton with its pier and Sumner are the better known ocean beaches. Godley Head Historic Reserve, Ferrymead Historic Park, Gondola and Antarctic Centre are other well known places of interest.

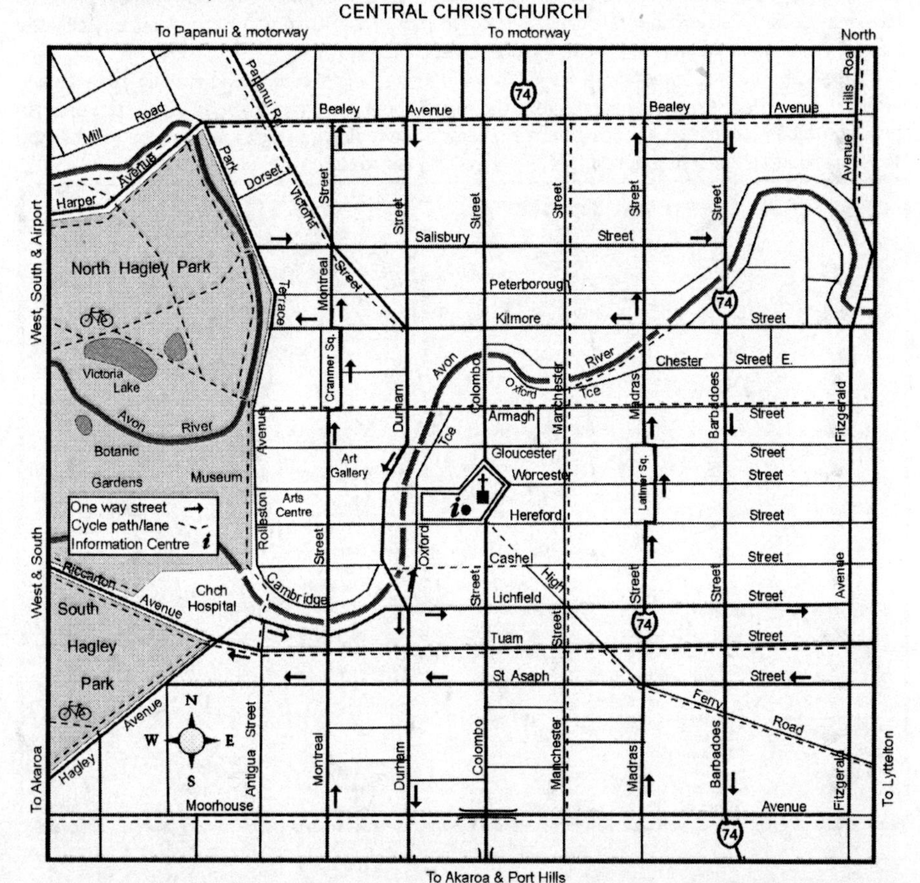

Opportunities for mountain biking with panoramic views of the city are had by going up to the PORT HILLS. They're reached using any one of several routes, the main two being . . .

Dyer's Pass Road at the south end of Colombo St, passing the fine gothic Sign of the Takahe (restaurant, devonshire teas) & Sign of the Kiwi (refreshments) joining Summit Rd or . . .

Evan's Pass Road is reached by going along Ferry Rd and through Sumner, at the opposite end of Summit Road. Both routes can be used to go to LYTTELTON PORT & HARBOUR with the historic Timeball Station. Continue around the harbour to GOVERNOR'S BAY. An extended trip can include: DIAMOND HARBOUR and PARAU (motor camp, shop) on south side of harbour.

NOTE: These trips involve some steep hill climbs and descents and can either be separate day trips, combined as one, or part of a journey to Banks Peninsula via Port Levy where the road becomes a steep rough gravel track arriving at Pigeon Bay. See Side Trip below for Banks Peninsula.

DIRECTIONS: These directions follow the main non-motorway routes into and out of the city and in most cases will be busy with other road users. There is a cycle street map available prduced by the city council, who are developing a number of cycle lanes and paths.

SOUTH From DUNEDIN: At the round-about just after the Sockburn Overbridge, take the third exit onto Blenheim Rd and continue to the round-about at the other end. At take the second exit (right) skirting Hagley Park to the left joining Moorhouse Ave. At first traffic lights go left onto Hagley Ave which flows into Oxford Terrace then Lichfield St. Go left (north) into Colombo St, arriving at Cathedral Square, visitor information is left (west) 1 block along Worcester St.

To DUNEDIN: From Cathedral Square head south along Colombo St, go right along Tuam St and through Hagley Park along Riccarton Ave to the round-about. Go straight ahead along Riccarton Rd through the busy Riccarton shopping centre. Follow Timaru direction signs taking care to cross the Sockburn round-about and overbridge. Continue along this road.

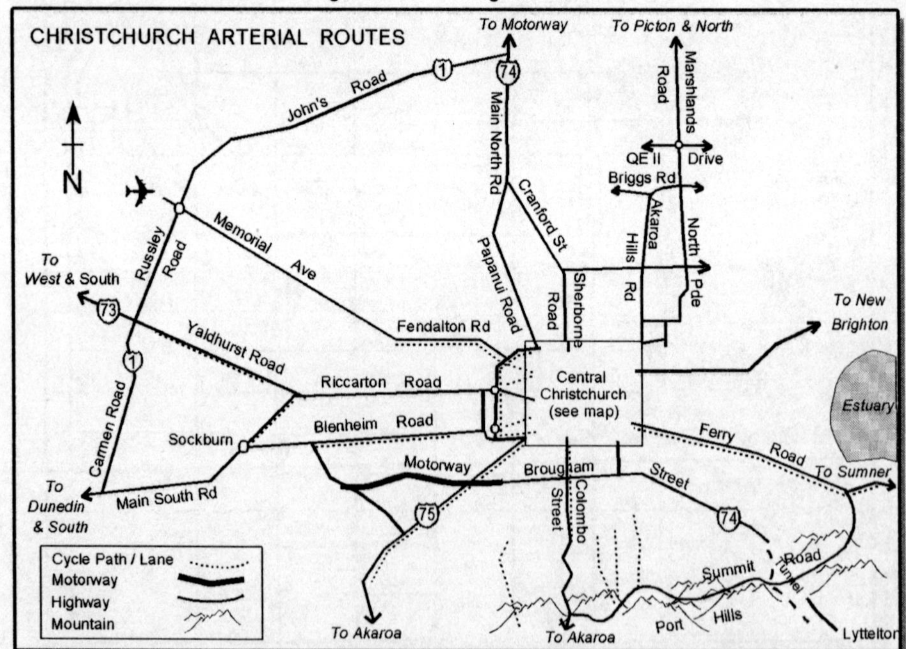

NORTH: From PICTON: Main North Rd changes at Kaiapoi to Marshlands Rd and then to North Pde. Take this route through to the end, going right (west) at the T junction along North Avon Rd, straight ahead to the T junction and left (south) into Whitmore St. At the first traffic lights turn right into Bealey Ave going 5 blocks then left into Colombo St. Cathedral Square is straight ahead.

To PICTON: Head north from Cathedral Square along Colombo St, go right (east) onto Bealey Ave, then left (north) at Whitmore St/Fitzgerald Ave. This becomes Hills Rd, Akaroa St, and Briggs Rd. Soon go left (north) onto Marshlands Rd and follow this, eventually arriving at Kaiapoi.

WEST & SOUTH WEST: From GREYMOUTH & QUEENSTOWN: Follow SH 73 through to the end of Yaldhurst Rd. At Church Corner bear left onto *Riccarton Rd, go straight through the busy Riccarton Shopping Centre to the round-about at Hagley Park. Take the second exit (straight) onto Riccarton Ave, bear left at the hospital onto Oxford Terrace joining Lichfield St. Go left (north) into Colombo St arriving at Cathedral Square, visitor information is in the Old Central Post Office under the clock tower.

To GREYMOUTH & QUEENSTOWN: From Cathedral Square head south along Colombo St going right along Tuam St and through Hagley Park along Riccarton Ave to the round-about. Go straight along Riccarton Rd through the busy *Riccarton shopping centre. Bear right at Church Corner onto Yaldhurst Rd and follow this out of the city and onto SH 73.

***NOTE:** An alternative to Riccarton Road is to go from Hagley Park to the airport along Fendalton Rd & Memorial Ave. At the round-about just before the airport go left along Russley Rd. At the next traffic lights go right onto Yaldhurst Road (SH 73). To go south follow the directions to Hororata at Aylesbury Corner or go left at Darfield, further along SH 73. To Arthurs Pass continue along SH 73. The Chch City Council has produced a cyclists street map.

1 SIDE TRIP: CHRISTCHURCH - AKAROA (Banks' Peninsula).

ROUTE:	SH 75	Summit Roads*
CHRISTCHURCH - AKAROA	83 km	98 km

* The middle section of Summit Rds joins SH 75 between Motukarara & Hilltop.

ALTERNATIVE CHCH - AKAROA. The busier, easier SH 75 via Taitapu and Duvauchelle or the quieter, scenic, more demanding Summit Roads. Both options meet at Motukarara, separate at Hilltop and meet again at Akaroa.

SIDE TRIP i PIGEON BAY, ii LITTLE AKALOA BAY, iii OKAINS BAY, iv LE BONS BAY.

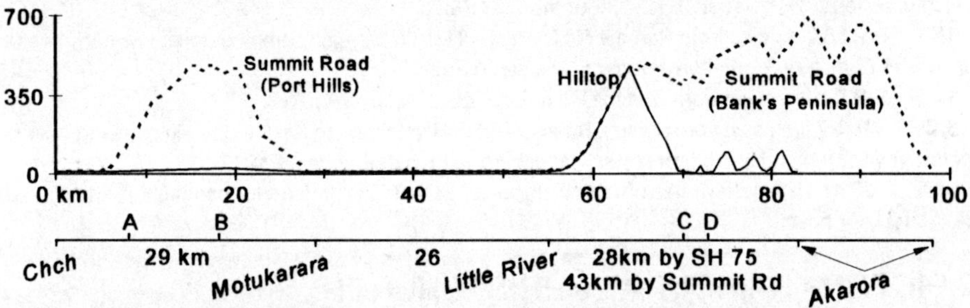

SERVICES: **CHRISTCHURCH:** See pages 7-11. **A) HALSWELL:** Store, pub.
B) TAITAPU: Store, pub. **MOTUKARARA:** Tearooms, domain camping (toilets, water, table).
ATAAHUA: Domain camping (toilets, water, table, shelter, tennis).
LITTLE RIVER: Alt 40m, pop 200. Takeaways/dairy/tearooms, pub, motor camp (5 km off SH 75).

HILLTOP: Alt 476m. Pub, tearooms. **C) BARRY'S BAY:** Cheese factory.
D) DUVAUCHELLE: Pop 150. Store, restaurant, pub, domain camping (no cabins); hotel/motel.
AKAROA: Altitude 10m ASL, population 1,700. ***i:*** 80 Rue Lavaud ☎304-8600.
Food: All outlets except supermarket. Accom: Motor camp; 4 bkpr hostel (incl 1 on farm); 4 motel; 2 hotel. Transport: Bus & shuttle to/from Chch. Week day mail bus to outer bays.

GRADIENTS: Via SH 75 from the Cathedral head south along Colombo St turning right into St Asaph St and bearing left along Hagley Ave. Cross Moorhouse Ave joining Lincoln Rd and the start of SH 75. This goes all the way to Akaroa. SH 75 skirts round the bottom of the Port Hills being mostly flat until Little River. Climb 8 km, 6 km quite steep & winding to the aptly named Hilltop (476m) and SH 75 & Summit Road junction. Drop 6 km of variable steepness to Barry's Bay and then rolls and undulates to Akaroa with four quite hard hills to cross, the last being the hardest.

ATTRACTIONS: Not much before Little River except Lake Ellesmere, a large area of water but only a few metres deep; really a lagoon, and Lake Forsyth. Swimming is not recommended due to serious pollution. In May 2006 part of the Little River Rail Trail opened between Motukarara and Little River. Summit Road traverses the crater rim of an extinct volcano. Fine views of the outer bays spreading like a fan on one side and long arms of the inner harbour on the other.

The principal settlement of Akaroa sits in the bottom of the ancient caldera. This is NZ's only French colony, established in 1840, now a pleasant village & tourist resort, including Canterbury's oldest house. It retains some of its Gallic essence with French named streets. The Banks Peninsula Track is a private walking track, starting at and returning to Akaroa. A few scenic reserves contain remnants of a native forest that once covered most of the peninsula. Sea fishing, kayaking, penguin spotting and swimming with dolphins are possibilities.

OPTIONS: **ALTERNATIVE** VIA SUMMIT ROADS. Head south from Cathedral Square being flat all the way along Colombo St to Dyers Pass Rd. Up steep from there passing SIGN of the TAKAHE (restaurant, devonshire teas) to SIGN of the KIWI (refreshments). Then continues up gradually before dropping along Gebbies Pass Rd and going right at the junction. Continue down eventually joining SH 75 at Motukarara and go left. Mostly flat until Little River then climb 8 km, 6 km quite steep & winding to the aptly named Hilltop (476m). Go left onto Summit Rd leaving SH 75. This narrow sealed road bobs and weaves along the lip of the crater. There are opportunities to drop down and explore the many bays of the outer harbour, see Side Trips below. Hilly. There is a final 600m descent in 6½ km into Akaroa, much of it steep. This way is 16 km longer than SH 75.

SIDE TRIP i 6 km down from Summit Rd to PIGEON BAY: Domain camping (toilets, water), hostel, access to Port Levy & Lyttelton along a rough steep track.

SIDE TRIP ii 8 km down from Summit Rd to LITTLE AKALOA BAY.

SIDE TRIP iii 7 km down from Summit Rd to OKAINS BAY: Store, museum, Domain camping (toilets, water, pavilion), bkpr hostel, farmstays. The village is 1 km before beach.

SIDE TRIP iv 10 km down from Summit Rd to LE BONS BAY: the motor camp/shop has closed, seasonal bkpr hostel.

2 PICTON - KAIKOURA - CHRISTCHURCH.

ROUTE:

	SH 1	SH 70/7/1
2a) PICTON - KAIKOURA	158 km	
2b) KAIKOURA - CHRISTCHURCH	187 km	203 km
Total	345 km	

ALTERNATIVE 2a) PICTON - BLENHEIM. The busier, easier SH 1 or the quiet, scenic & mostly gravel Port Underwood Road. Both options meet near Spring Creek.

2b) KAIKOURA - WAIPARA. The busier, easier SH 1 via Cheviot or the quiet scenic but difficult, SH 70 through Waiau. See page 14.

SIDE TRIP 2a) i LAKE GRASSMERE - MARFELLS BEACH. ii To SAW CUT GORGE.

2b) i CHEVIOT - GORE BAY - PORT ROBINSON. ii GRETA VALLEY - MOTANAU BEACH.

2b Alt) CLARENCE RESERVE CONSERVATION AREA.

LINK ROAD 2a) i BLENHEIM - ST ARNAUD on sealed SH 63. See Page 67.

ii DASHWOOD (SH 1) - MOLESWORTH STATION - HANMER SPRINGS (SH 7).

2b) WOODEND (SH 1) - RANGIORA - OXFORD (SH 72) - SHEFFIELD (SH 73).

2a PICTON - BLENHEIM - KAIKOURA. 158km

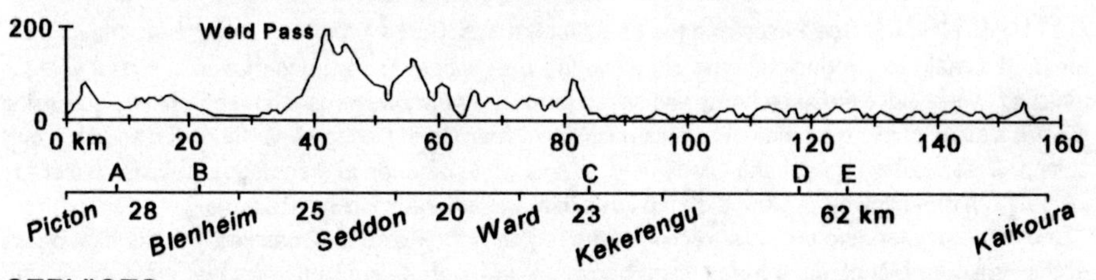

SERVICES: **PICTON:** Altitude 30m ASL, population 4,000. ***i:*** The Foreshore ☎573-7477.
Food: All outlets. Accom: 5 motor camp; hostel (7 bkpr, 1 YHA); 10 motel; 4 hotel.
Transport: Ferry to/from Wellington. Train to/from Chch. Bus & shuttles to/from Nelson & Chch.
A) KOROMIKO: Store, motel. **B) SPRING CREEK:** Store, motor camp, hotel. **GROVETOWN:** Hotel.
BLENHEIM: Alt 10m, pop 19,000. ***i:*** Queen St ☎578-9904. Food: All outlets.
Accom: 3 motor camp; 6 bkpr hostel; 9 motel; 5 hotel. Bicycle shops.
SEDDON: Alt 95 m, pop 550. Store, tearooms, takeaways, pub. Motor camp, bkpr hostel.
WARD: Alt 35m, pop 200. Dairy/tearooms, pub. Motel (possible camping also).
C) URE/WAIMA RIVER: Cyclists' hostel (also camping & small shop), 1½ km up Ure Road. See below for details. **KEKERENGU:** Tearooms. **D) CLARENCE RIVER:** picnic area.
E) WAIPAPA BAY: DoC Motor camp (no cabins or kitchen). **HAPUKU RIVER:** picnic area.
KAIKOURA: Alt 15m, pop 2,600. ***i:*** The Esplanade ☎319-5641. Food: All outlets.
Accom: Motor camp 3; hostel (8 bkpr, 1 YHA); 12 motel; 3 hotel. Bicycle shop.
Transport: Train to/from Chch & Picton. Bus & shuttles to/from Chch & Picton.

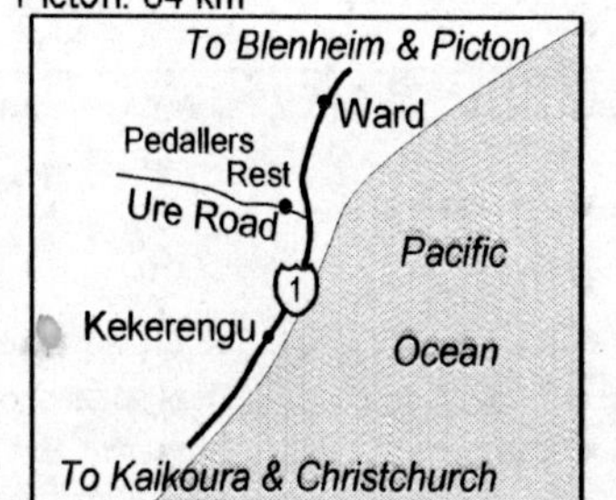

GRADIENTS: Apart from a moderate climb out of Picton, SH 1 has mostly easy gradients through to Blenheim and continues flat for another 8 km beyond. Then a long gradual 6½ km climb starts becoming steeper and winding for the last 2½ km to Weld Pass (196m). Then follows a gradual descent and short ascent to Dashwood Pass (163m), ending with a long 3½ km quite steep drop. SH 1 then levels out to undulate with a short dip and rise to cross Awatere River before arriving at Seddon.

Departing Seddon the 11 km to Lake Grassmere are rolling with two larger hills to cross, from where the terrain becomes easier for the last part to Ward. Rolling country after Ward(!) ending with a 1 km climb and a 2 km gradual descent to join the coas t at Waima (Ure) River. The road then undulates along a narrow shelf, Pacific Ocean to the left, cliffs to the right, with no more difficult hills before Kaikoura. Only the last 11 of the 74 km from Waima River leave the coast to roll across the plains around Kaikoura. Apart from an hour before and after the ferry sails, SH 1 traffic flows are usually light.

ATTRACTIONS: See Picton and the beautiful Sounds. Sunny Blenheim and Wairau Plains have an ideal climate for producing some of the world's best wines. The transformation in recent years is amazing, where once stood orchards and sheep farms are now vineyards, boom boom! Not surprising NZ has a binge drinking problem. En route pass the historic Cobb Cottage near Blenheim and NZ's only solar powered salt works at Lake Grassmere, whose white mounds and sometimes pinkish water are visible from the highway. A short side trip goes to Marfells Beach Scenic Reserve.

One of the outstanding scenic attraction of the region is the Kaikoura Coastline with the high peaks of the Kaikoura Mountains a magnificent backdrop. In Maori Kaikoura means "eat crayfish" and an abundance of marine life just off shore in the deep Kaikoura Trench provides a variety of seafood to sample. Whales are not on the menu yet but watching them is, as is swimming with dolphins. Added attractions include tramping, horse trekking & sniffing the local seal colony.

OPTIONS: **ALTERNATIVE** PICTON - BLENHEIM via PORT UNDERWOOD along a scenic but rough, narrow, gravel, winding, in short, difficult road! Beware of logging trucks. DoC camping at WHITE'S BEACH and WHATAMONGA BAY both have toilets and water, otherwise no services. Rejoin SH 1 at Spring Creek just north of Blenheim.

SIDE TRIP i LAKE GRASSMERE - MARFELLS BEACH: DoC camping (toilet, table, water). Off SH 1 for 8 km east along the south side of Lake Grassmere on an easy, partly gravel road.

SIDE TRIP ii To the aptly named SAW CUT GORGE Scenic Reserve up Ure/Waima River Road passing Pedallers Rest cyclists hostel.

LINK ROAD DASHWOOD - MOLESWORTH STATION - HANMER SPRINGS See page 27.

2b KAIKOURA - WAIPARA - CHRISTCHURCH. 187km

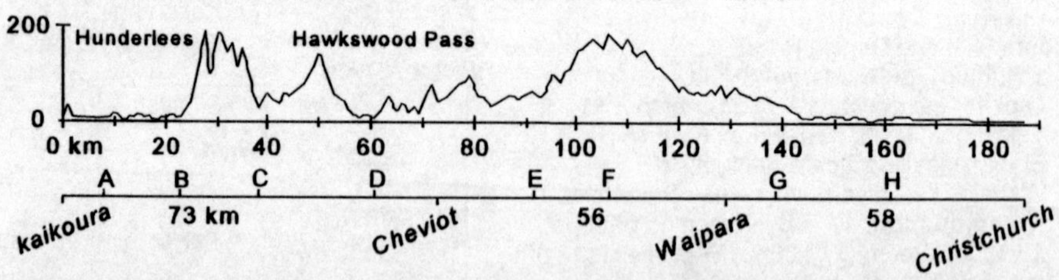

SERVICES: **KAIKOURA:** See previous section. **A) PEKETA BAY:** Motor Camp (small shop). **GOOSE BAY:** DoC motor camp has small shop, across railway track adjacent SH 1. They also manage other DoC camping/picnic areas nearby. **B) OARO:** Alt 10m. Tearooms/Motel, cabins.

5.30am

OKARAHIA STREAM: picnic area (table). **C) CONWAY RIVER:** Alt 80m picnic area.
HAWKSWOOD: Alt 145m, farm hostel/camp. **D) WAIAU RIVER:** Alt 45m picnic area.
CHEVIOT: Alt 46m, pop 1,000. Food: All outlets except supermarket.
Accom: Motels (also tent sites & cabin); hotel (also tent sites). **DOMETT:** Small shop in petrol station.
E) HURUNUI RIVER: picnic area. **F) GRETA VALLEY:** Alt 180m. Store, pub/restaurant/motor camp.
WAIPARA: Alt 60m, pop 270. Tearooms, hotel/restaurant, store, bkpr hostel.
G) AMBERLEY: Alt 30m, pop 900. Store, tearooms, takeaways, dairy, pub. Motel/caravan park. Beach motor camp 5 km E of SH 1. **LEITHFIELD:** Beach motor camp with small shop, 2 km E of SH 1.
WAIKUKU: Beach motor camp with small shop, 3 km E of SH 1.
H) WOODEND: Alt 10m, pop 1,000. Food: Tearooms, takeaways, dairy, restaurant, pub.
Accom: Motor camp/shop/restaurant (3 km S at Main North Rd/motorway junction). Motor camp with small shop at beach, (no cabins), 3 km E of SH 1. 2 motel.
KAIAPOI: Alt 10m, pop 5,500. All types of food outlets. Motor camp (no kitchen); motel. Bicycle shop.
CHRISTCHURCH: See page 7-9.

GRADIENTS: After climbing the small hill to leave Kaikoura, SH 1 resumes its gentle undulations, rejoining the coast at Peketa Bay for the 14 kms to Oaro. After Oaro the highway heads inland to cross the Hunderlees, three sometimes steep and winding hills in 15 km, the first and last being the steepest, reaching 200m and descending to 100m. After the Conway River is a long gradual ascent to Hawkswood Pass (145m), with a gradual drop and gradients easing to a gentle descent to Waiau River, followed by moderate rolls into Cheviot.

The terrain is of a mostly gentle nature from Cheviot with only a few hills, mainly to cross watersheds of minor rivers, continuing the same until 6 km south of Greta Valley. Undulations to Waipara and after which SH 1 flattens as it approaches Amberley. Cyclists are prohibited on the motorway, so 3 km south of Woodend bear left onto Main North Rd to Kaiapoi. See next section for directions into Christchurch.

ATTRACTIONS: The coast south of Kaikoura is as spectacular as its northern counterpart and has several scenic reserves around Goose Bay. St Anne's Lagoon & Cheviot Hills Domain are pleasant spots near Cheviot and a few scenic areas dot the adjacent shoreline, see Options (side trips i & ii) below. Side trips go to several beach resorts along the coast to the east of SH 1 between Waipara and Christchurch. The Canterbury Plains begin with a vengeance, having hardly a bump or bend and only increasingly heavy traffic to excite the passing pedalist! Take care on the shoulderless bridges. Sheep stations are being rapidly replaced by dairy farms so swimming in the lowland rivers the highway passes is no longer recommended, due to effluent and nutrient run-off.

OPTIONS: **SIDE TRIP i** 8 km along an easy sealed road from Cheviot to the small settlement of GORE BAY: Domain camping (water, toilets, coin showers, no cabins or kitchen). A sealed road, steep in places, links Gore Bay with HURUNUI RIVER MOUTH Domain camping (toilets, water, donation payment). Nearby CATHEDRAL CLIFFS & PORT ROBINSON WALKWAY are the local attractions. Return to SH 1 the same way or directly to Domett along a sealed road from Hurunui River Mouth or rejoin SH 1 along Blythe Rd S of Domett. Confused? So am I! Then seek local help.

SIDE TRIP ii GRETA VALLEY - MOTUNAU BEACH: Domain camping (water, toilets) no cabins, a seaside village 16 km from SH 1, hilly at both ends. A wildlife refuge is off the coast at Motunau Island.

2b ALTERNATIVE: KAIKOURA - WAIAU - WAIPARA. 145km

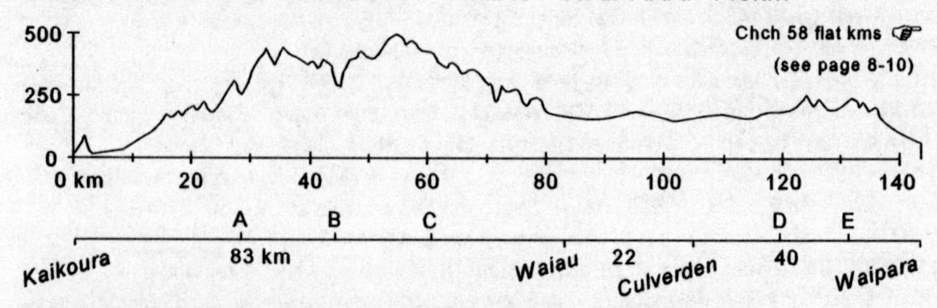

SERVICES: **KAIKOURA:** See page 11. Note: No shops for 83 km to Waiau.
A) GREEN BURN: picnic area. **B) CONWAY RIVER:** picnic area.
C) Mt LYFORD: Hotel with bkpr accom and restaurant.
WAIAU: Alt 150m, pop 230. Store, takeaways, tearooms, hotel, motor camp.
ROTHERHAM: Store, hotel. **CULVERDEN:** Alt 175m, pop 400. Store, takeaways/tearooms, pub, motel.
BALMORAL FOREST: DoC style camping (toilet, table, water). **D) HURUNUI:** Alt 190m. Hotel.
E) WAIKARI: Alt 220m. Tearooms (seasonal) pub, inexpensive cyclists homestay, (see page 26) for details, domain camping. **WAIPARA:** Alt 60m, pop 270. Tearooms, restaurant, store, bkpr hostel, hotel.
CHRISTCHURCH: See pages 7-9.

GRADIENTS: This is 16 km longer than SH 1. 5½ km south of Kaikoura go right onto SH 70 and start a 12 km uphill that becomes steeper tpwards the end. It is a good warm-up for the hills to come! Although there are a few flattish bits, much of the highway to Waiau is of a hilly nature as it dips into one river valley and climbs over the hill to the next. Of particular note are out of Kuhutaru Stream, Green Burn, Conway River and past Doone Graveyard, where there are 100m plus climbs! Gradients ease from 4km before Waiau all the way through to Hurunui. Then a few moderate rolls through Waikari and Weka Pass before a moderate rolling downhill eases to a gentle descent as SH 7 joins SH1 at Waipara. The highest point is 511m at Whales Back Saddle, about 5½ km east of Mt Lyford turn-off.

ATTRACTIONS: SH 70 was called the Inland kaikoura Road but is now Pacific Alpine Triangle? Solitude is the main attraction with isolated sheep stations and riverside picnic areas. Pass historic sites such as Doone Graveyard. About 25km south of Kaikoura a side trip goes to Clarence Reserve, a remote area of the Clarence River Valley between Seaward and Inland Kaikoura mountains, vehicles are prohibited. A place for keen mountain bikers, see DoC's brochure for details. Another side trip goes to Mt Lyford ski village, established in1988. Waiau is a rural village that has seen better days. Pass the historic hotel at Hurunui and goat-like Frog Rock in scenic Weka Pass on the way to Waipara.

SIDE TRIP To CLARENCE RESERVE A huge remote area of the Clarence River Valley between the Seaward and Inland Kaikoura Mountains. Out of bounds to vehicles. A place for keen mountain bikers See DoC's brochure for details. Turn off SH 70 about 25km south of Kaikoura. No services.

LINK ROAD WOODEND (SH 1) - OXFORD - SHEFFIELD (SH 73) on SH 72. Distance 57 km.

Either direct on SH 72 or along an alternative skirting Mt Thomas. Both routes are sealed with a gradual climb as they head inland. Mostly rural countryside & towns. Leave Woodend passing through: RANGIORA: Alt 30m, pop 6,000. All types of food outlets. Motor camp & 2 motel. Bicycle shop. Then OXFORD: Alt 235m, pop 1,000. Food: All outlets except supermarket. Accom: Bkpr hostel.
Cross the Waimakariri River Bridge before arriving at SH 73. & SHEFFIELD: Alt 300m, Pub.

Alternatively from Rangiora go 5 km N to ASHLEY (hotel) then LOBURN (motor camp), followed by MT THOMAS: DoC camping (toilet, water, table) then ASHLEY GORGE (motor camp/shop). This way is 11 km longer than SH 72 but is more interesting with slight side trips to Ashley Gorge & Mt Thomas.

3 CHRISTCHURCH - TIMARU - DUNEDIN.

ROUTE:	SH 1
3a) CHCH - ASHBURTON - TIMARU	163 km
3b) TIMARU - OAMARU - DUNEDIN	200 km
Total	363 km

Note: If time allows a more interesting option goes inland through the MacKenzie Country and Waitaki Valley from Chch to Oamaru. See pages 32-37.

ALTERNATIVE 3b) i HOOK - WAIMATE on SH 82.
ii OAMARU - DUNEDIN. The busier SH 1 or quieter, more interesting Kakanui Coast, Trotter's Gorge & Karitane Coast routes. Both options meet several times. See page 18.

LINK ROAD 3a) i RAKAIA (SH 1) - THOMPSON TRACK - MAYFIELD (SH 72). See page 16.
ii RANGITATA (SH 1) - GERALDINE on SH 79. iii TIMARU - FAIRLIE on SH 8. See page 16.
3b) i OAMARU (SH 1) - OMARAMA (SH 8) on SH 83. See page 37.
ii PALMERSTON (SH 1) - RANFURLY on SH 85. See page 22.

3a CHRISTCHURCH - ASHBURTON - TIMARU. 163km

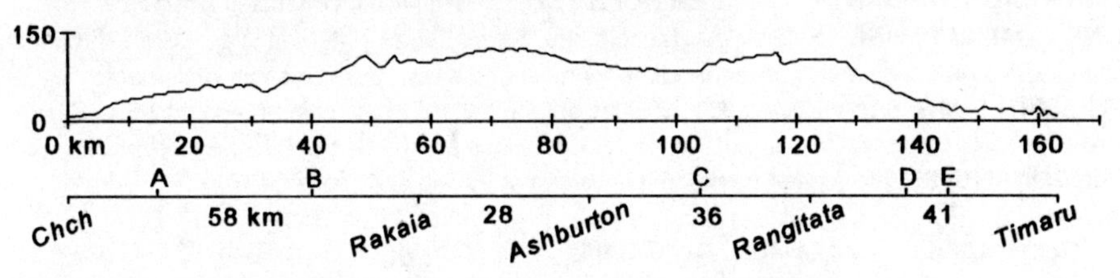

SERVICES: **CHRISTCHURCH:** See pages7-9. **A) TEMPLETON:** Dairy, tearooms, pub.
ROLLESTON: Altitude 55m, pub. **BURNHAM:** Alt 65m, pub, army camp.
SELWYN RIVER: Restaurant, picnic area. **B) DUNSANDEL:** Store, tearooms, pub.
RAKAIA: Alt 105m, pop 800. Store, takeaways, tearooms, pub, motor camp. **DROMORE:** picnic area.
ASHBURTON: Alt 90m, pop 15,000. ***i:*** East St ☎308-1064. Food: All outlets.
Accom: 2 motor camp; bkpr hostel; 8 motel; hotel. Bicycle Shop.
WINSLOW: picnic area. **C) HINDS:** Alt 80m, pop 300. Store, pub. **EALING:** picnic area.
RANGITATA: Alt 105m. Tearooms/cabins. Motor camp (S bank of river mouth, no cabins).

ORARI: Farm motor camp (off SH 1 towards Geraldine).
D) WINCHESTER: Alt 40m, pop 270. Shop in petrol station.
Accom: Domain motor camp (no cabins, open Labour W/E to May); motel; hotel.
E) TEMUKA: Alt: 20m, pop 3,900. Food: All outlets. Accom: Motor camp; 3 motel; 2 hotel.
TIMARU: Altitude 10m, pop 28,000. ***i:*** Landing Services Building, George St ☎688-6163.
Food: All outlets. Accom: 3 motor camp; 2 bkpr hostel; 16 motel; 8 hotel. Bicycle shops.
Transport: Bus & shuttles to/from Dunedin, Qutn & Chch. Thrice weekly summer shuttle to/from Mt Cook (who also give 10% off with this book).

GRADIENTS: Almost flat for 163 km to Timaru apart from a noticeable drop at Rangitata to cross the river. Beware the long narrow, shoulderless bridges of the Rakaia and Rangitata Rivers, the former is the longest in NZ at nearly 2 kms. Elevation rarely climbs above 100m over the entire route. Can be demoralising in headwinds. Often busy with lots of fast cars and large trucks.

ATTRACTIONS: Cross the bridges of the broad braided rivers that drain the flat Canterbury Plains. SH 1 travels near the coast but never touching it until Timaru. Most towns and villages service the surrounding rural communities. Rakaia town centre has a giant salmon (or perhaps it's a trout) and the adjcent Rakaia River is popular for fishing. At Upper Waitohi, near Temuka, is a memorial to local boy Richard Pearce who in 1903. may have beaten the Wright Brothers as the first to achieve powered (but uncontrolled) flight.

Otherwise, apart from the odd short walkway or minor historic site there is little to interest the passing cyclist, unless a fisherman or sheep fetish. A place to escape mass market tourists! Timaru is a bustling port city and has the annual Caroline Bay Carnival during the summer school holidays.

OPTIONS: A number of highways head inland from SH 1 to join the Chch to Queenstown route (see Central, pages 32/33 for onward travel). All have barely noticeable climbs, the main ones being:

LINK ROAD i RAKAIA - MAYFIELD on THOMPSON TRACK. No services. Distance 53 km.
LINK ROAD ii RANGITATA - ORARI BRIDGE on SH79, no services. Distance 9 km.
LINK ROAD iii TIMARU - FAIRLIE. Distance 62km. 6 km north of Timaru at Washdyke SH 8 heads inland with a gradual, barely noticeable climb for most of the way, passing small settlements.
PLEASANT POINT: Alt 65m, pop 1,000. All types of food outlets. Motor camp (Labour W/E to Easter).
CAVE: Alt 155m, pop 100. Store, pub. Maori rock drawings nearby. ALBURY: Alt 225m, pop 80, pub.
TENGAWAI RIVER: picnic area (table). Finally arrive at Fairlie, see pages 34.

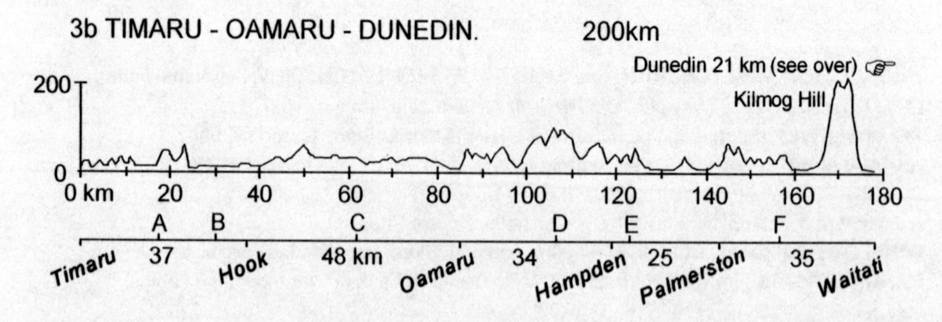

SERVICES: **TIMARU:** See above for details. **PAREORA:** Dairy.
A) St ANDREWS: Alt 50m. Store, tearooms, pub. Domain camping. **B) MAKIKIHI:** Store, hotel.
HOOK: Tearooms. **C) GLENAVY:** Alt 30m, pop 170. Store, pub. Motor camp 3, Hotel.
WAITAKI RIVER: picnic area (toilets, water, table) on north bank. **HILDERTHORPE:** Pub.
OAMARU: Alt 10m, pop 13,000. ***i:*** 1 Thames St ☎434-1656. Food: All outlets.
Accom: Motor camp; hostel (3 bkpr, 1 YHA (Oct to April); 11 motel; hotel.
Transport: Several bus & shuttles to/from Chch, Dunedin & Waimate. Thrice weekly shuttle to/from Mt Cook gives 10% off with this book. Bicycle shops. **MAHENO:** Store.
D) HERBERT: Alt 50m, pop 350. Store. DoC camping (toilet, table, water, gas bbq) 2 km W of SH 1. Domain camping (toilet, water, table) about 2 km S of Herbert.
WAIANAKARUA: Bkpr hostel/camping, restaurant, picnic area. **KAKAHO RIVER:** picnic area.
HAMPDEN: Alt 50m, pop 300. Store, takeaways, pub. Motor camp, motel.
MOERAKI BOULDERS: Tearooms. **E) MOERAKI VILLAGE:** Alt 30m, pop 140. Motor camp; motel.
KATIKI BEACH: Two picnic area (at each end of the beach).
PALMERSTON: Alt 20m, pop 900. Food: All outlets except supermarket.
Accom: Motor camp (3 km S) has closed; motel; 2 hotel.
F) WAIKOUAITI: Alt 30m, pop 900. Store, dairy, takeaways, tearooms, pub. Motor camp; motel 2.
WAIKOUAITI RIVER: picnic area (table). **EVANSDALE:** Tearooms/store. **WAITATI:** Store.
DUNEDIN See next section for details.

GRADIENTS: Becomes rolling over low hills after Timaru until Hook but nothing too difficult, then returns to almost flat country again from there to Oamaru. Climb the hill out of Oamaru, the start of long rolling hills alternating with easier gradients to Moeraki. Mostly gentle gradients from there until Palmerston apart from a small hill south end of Katiki Beach. Rolling hills from Palmerston (beware the narrow Tumai Overbridge) until Karitane turn off, south of Waikouaiti. A short distance beyond here the Kilmog Hill starts, a long, sometimes steep climb of 5½ km to 225m followed by a steep 3 km descent. Flat from Evansdale for 3½ km to Waitati. The motorway starts here, so take Mt Cargill Rd.

ATTRACTIONS: The low hills of North Otago take over from the flat Canterbury Plains, still heavily populated by sheep. Continue travelling near the coast but still rarely seeing it. A short detour inland goes to the pleasant village of Waimate (see options below) complete with a couple of scenic reserves and White Horse on the hill. Pukeuri has a freezing works, is on the 45th parallel, junction for SH 83 going inland to Mt Cook and not much else.

Oamaru has several attractions including the usual walks, the Whitestone Historical Conservation Area (a collection of Victorian buildings), excellent botanic gardens and yellow eyed and little blue penguin colonies (in season). The latter are clever little critters, they've built a grandstand and visitor centre and employ humans to collect money from people watching them return to their nests. Every November there is a heritage festival featuring New Zealand's Penny Farthing Cycle Championships.

Further south are more historical attractions; Totara Estate, Clark's Mill, Waianakarua Bridge and Millhouse. Look out for the giant man (& woman) eating bird (and egg) adjacent SH 1 at Waianakarua just after the bridge, waiting to pounce on passing pedallers!! Beyond are Moeraki Boulders (Devil's Marbles) and village with nearby yellow-eyed penguins; Katiki Beach and Shag Point. Pass quaint villages such as Herbert and Waikouaiti, perhaps see a rare royal spoonbill in the lagoon here. Access the Pigroot from Palmerston inland to Ranfurly.

NOTE: Kakanui Coast, Trotter's Gorge & Karitane Coast are pretty, quieter alternatives to SH 1 to Dunedin. See Alternative ii below.

OPTIONS: **ALTERNATIVE i** HOOK - WAIMATE Join SH 82 going the 9 km to the rural town of WAIMATE: Alt 55m, pop 3,000. Food: All outlets. Accom: Motor camp; Domain camping (toilet, water, table, hot showers, no cabins); motel 2; hotel 2. Bicycle shop.

There are three scenic reserves nearby; Kelcey's, Gunn's and Hook Bush, informal camping may be possible. See the White Horse of Waimate, a memorial to the Clydesdale horses, on the hill side above the town in the direction of Kelcey's Bush (Farm camp, no cabins).

Return 6 km to SH 1 heading south in the direction of Oamaru & Dunedin. Alternatively SH 82 continues inland past WAIHAO FORKS: (hotel) joining SH 83 at KUROW heading up the Waitaki Valley, see page 37.

ALTERNATIVE ii OAMARU - DUNEDIN weaves across SH 1 as follows.

KAKANUI COAST: From Oamaru head up Severn St, at the top bear left onto Awamoa Rd and continue until the T junction. Go left on to Thousand Acre Road and on reaching the coast go right to KAKANUI (store, bkpr hostel, domain camping) and ALL DAY BAY (bkpr hostel). Mostly easy gradients and staying with the shoreline much of the way. Rejoin SH 1 at the historic Waianakarua River Bridge & Millhouse. Go left onto SH 1 for 15 km passing the big bird & Moeraki Boulders. Shortlly after Moeraki Village turn off go right onto:

HORSE RANGE ROAD: Pass the secluded TROTTER'S GORGE Scenic Reserve, 5 km along Horse Range Rd, then right down a track for a short distance and ford a stream. After the gorge there is a 190m climb in 3 km to the HORSE RANGE SADDLE (240m) with a 2 km gravel section just past the summit. A twisting descent before levelling out for the last bit into PALMERSTON, 9 km S of the saddle. Rejoin SH 1 for another 18 km. Go left after Waikouaiti to. . . .

KARITANE COAST: This avoids the Kilmog Hill but has plenty of ups and downs of its own with one very steep climb just after Karitane and splendid views. Pass the holiday villages of KARITANE (dairy, motor camp), SEACLIFF (bkpr hostel) & WARRINGTON: picnic area (toilets), before rejoining SH 1 at Evansdale. Directions for the last 21 km into Dunedin are in the next section.

LINK ROAD i OAMARU - OMARAMA (SH 8) on (SH 83). See page 37.

LINK ROAD ii PALMERSTON (SH 1) - KYEBURN (SH 87) near Ranfurly on SH 85. See page 22.

4 DUNEDIN AND OTAGO PENINSULA.

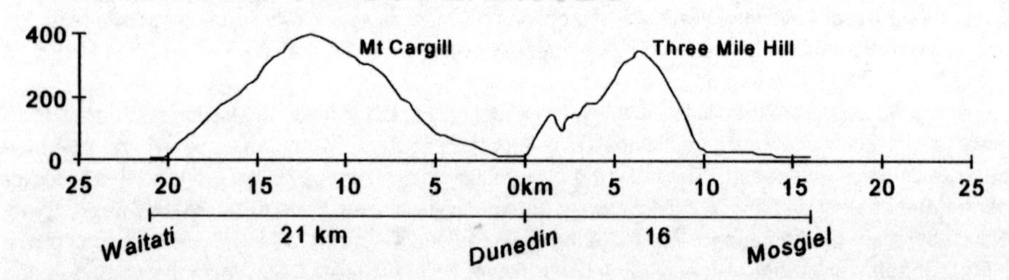

SERVICES: **DUNEDIN:** Altitude 50m, population 114,000. ***i:*** 48, The Octagon ☎474-3300.
Food: Many of all types of outlets. Accom: 3 motor camp; hostel (7 bkpr, 1 YHA); lots motel; many hotel. Transport: Bus & shuttles to/from Invercargill, Queenstown, Te Anau & Chch. Shuttle to/from the Catlins. Bicycle shops.

OTAGO PENINSULA: McANDREW BAY: Store, takeaways.
PORTABELLO: Store, pub, motor camp, bkpr hostel. LARNACH CASTLE: Lodge.

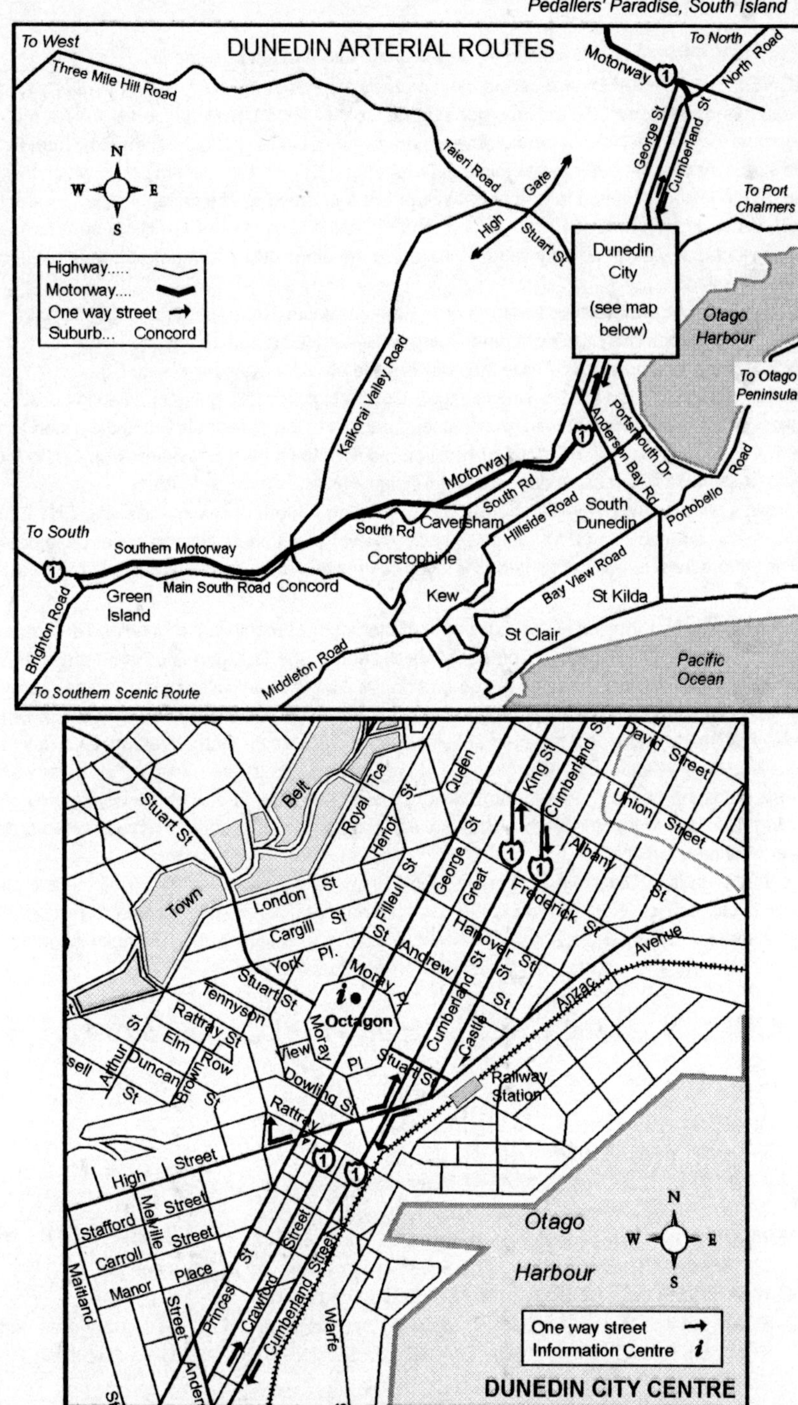
DUNEDIN ARTERIAL ROUTES
To West
Three Mile Hill Road
To North
Motorway
North Road
George St
Cumberland St
Taieri Road
High
Gate
Stuart St
To Port Chalmers
Dunedin City (see map below)
Highway.....
Motorway....
One way street
Suburb... Concord
Otago Harbour
To Otago Peninsula
Kaikorai Valley Road
Portsmouth Dr
Anderson Bay Rd
Motorway
South Rd
Road
Portobello
South Dunedin
Hillside Road
South Rd
Caversham
To South
Southern Motorway
Corstophine
Bay View Road
Main South Road
Concord
Green Island
Kew
St Kilda
Brighton Road
St Clair
Middleton Road
Pacific Ocean
To Southern Scenic Route
Stuart St
Belt
Royal
Tce
Heriot
St
Queen
St
King St
Cumberland St
David Street
Union Street
Albany
St
Town
London St
Cargill St
Filleul St
George St
Great
Frederick St
Hanover St
York Pl.
Moray Pl.
Andrew St
Stuart St
Tennyson
Octagon
Cumberland St
Castle
Avenue
Anzac
Rattray St
Arthur St
Elm Row
Duncan
Brown St
View
Moray
Pl
Stuart St
Railway Station
Dowling St
Rattray
High Street
Stafford Street
Melville Street
Carroll Street
Manor Place
Maitland
Street
Princes St
Crawford Street
Cumberland Street
Warfe
Otago Harbour
One way street
Information Centre
DUNEDIN CITY CENTRE

DIRECTIONS: Very hilly whichever way is taken into and out of Dunedin.

NORTH: From OAMARU. Just before the motorway, turn off at WAITATI taking Mt Cargill Rd. A long sometimes quite steep 8½ km climb goes up Mt Cargill (400m), then descends for 7 km of variable steepness, before easing to a gentle down and arriving in Dunedin along North Rd. North Rd passes Baldwin St. At the first traffic lights join the Cumberland St one way system along which a cycle lane runs. At the Railway Station turn right onto Stuart St and arrive at The Octagon after 3 short blocks.

SOUTH & WEST: To QUEENSTOWN & INVERCARGILL: A steep 1 km climb up Stuart St begins from the Octagon with an equally steep ½ km down the other side. From here there is a choice of two routes as follows.....

To Southern Scenic Route: bear left onto Kaikorai Valley Road and after a gentle 4 km descent, pass under the motorway. Go right, undulating to Green Island and shortly after bear left to Brighton.

To Mosgiel and Outram via Three Mile Hill: Instead of taking Kaikorai Valley Road join Taieri Rd to Mosgiel. Suburbia ends 4 km from the Octagon with the highway rolling and undulating uphill until Taieri Lookout picnic area (350m). It then drops, steep for much of the Three Mile Hill to the Taieri Plain, from where it becomes mostly flat. At SH 87 junction, go right to Outram & Middlemarch, left to Mosgiel. It is also possible to reach Lake Waihola and Sinclair Wetlands through Outram.

Note: It's possible to go from Dunedin to Mosgiel through South Dunedin and using SH1 from Green Island, such as South Rd or Portsmouth Drive/Bay View Rd. Unfortunately it is either quite complicated and/or suffers from heavy traffic. It is for those reasons this route hasn't been included here.

ATTRACTIONS: Known as the Edinburgh of the South, Dunedin is the Mainland's second biggest city and is an important cultural and educational centre. The Octagon is at the heart of this vibrant university city with plenty of things to see and do. Mt Cargill Scenic Reserve is on the route from the north and has spectacular views of Otago Harbour & Peninsula. On the way, try to cycle up Baldwin St, officially the world's steepest street at 38°. Take the scenic Taieri Gorge Railway as a day excursion or use it on the way to/from Central Otago. Culture vultures can try the museum, art gallery and newly opened NZ Sport Hall of Fame in the railway station. The latter is one of the city's many distinctive buildings. Guided tours of Speight's Brewery are popular, hick! Cadbury's have opened a chocolate museum at their factory.

A side trip goes to Otago Peninsula, either by bus or bike. The main attractions there are Larnach Castle & Glenfalloch, Fort Taiaroa & the disappearing gun, Taiaroa Head Nature Reserve with the Royal Albatross Colony and a yellow-eyed penguin colony. The aptly named Highcliff Rd that traverses a ridge of the old volcano and has spectacular views from the top.

5 DUNEDIN - RANFURLY - CROMWELL (Queenstown).

ROUTE:	SH 87/85/8
5a) DUNEDIN - RANFURLY	146 km
5b) RANFURLY - QUEENSTOWN	173 km
Total	319 km

ALTERNATIVE 5a & b) MIDDLEMARCH - CLYDE. SH 87 & SH 85 or gravel Otago Central Rail Trail.
5b) ii IDABURN - OMAKAU on SH 85 or Ida Valley Road. See page 23.

SIDE TRIP 5b) BECKS - ST BATHANS - LAUDER. See page 23.

LINK ROAD 5a) KYEBURN (SH 87) - PALMERSTON (SH 1) on SH 85, the Pigroot. See page 22.
5b) RANFURLY (SH 85) - DANSEY PASS - DUNTROON (SH 83) See page 23.

5a DUNEDIN - MIDDLEMARCH - RANFURLY. 146km

600
300
0
Dunedin 16 km
(see over)
Rail Trail
0 km 20 40 60 80 100 120
A B C D
Mosgiel 11 Outram 54 km Middlemarch 65 Ranfurly

SERVICES: **DUNEDIN:** See previous section.
MOSGIEL: Alt 10m, pop 9,200. Food: All outlets. Accom: Motel; hotel. Bicycle Shop.
OUTRAM: Alt 17m, pop 500. Store, pub. **A) CLARKE'S JUNCTION:** Alt 540m, Pub.
MIDDLEMARCH: Alt 200m, pop 200. Store with bkpr accom, pub, motor camp with bkpr accom.
B) MEMORIAL: picnic area. **HYDE:** Tearooms/bkpr accom. **C) KOKONGA:** picnic area.
WAIPIATA: Pub, Seasonal farm hostel 12 km S of Ranfurly, off SH 87 & West of Kokonga (closed).
D) KYEBURN: picnic area.
RANFURLY: Alt 425m, pop 950. Food: All outlets except supermarket.
Accom: Motor camp; motel; hotel (also bkpr beds). Transport: Shuttle to/from Dunedin & Queenstown.

GRADIENTS: Gentle gradients from Mosgiel until 2 km after Outram when SH 87 climbs long and steep for much of the next 5½ km. The steepness eases near the top and rolling country begins, some quite long and steep to Lee Stream. Rolling uphill from there until 5 km before Clarke's Junction when the gradients ease to undulating. Continues the same for another 2 km then plunges steeply for 2 km to cross the aptly named Deep Stream before climbing just as steeply for another 2 km. This is the first and hardest of three depressions in 17 km, the others are Shannon & Sutton Streams. After climbing out of the last hole there is a moderate descent into Middlemarch, the last 8 km being gentle.

The most difficult hills before Middlemarch can be avoided and the above description rendered useless by taking the Taieri Gorge railway from Dunedin to Pukerangi and a 20 km, partly gravel and occasional steep ride to Middlemarch. After Middlemarch SH 87 rolls and undulates much of the way to Ranfurly. Between Hyde and Teroiti the gradients get steeper and longer. If using the Rail Trail, the recommended section is between either the train accident memorial or Hyde and Kokonga or Waipiata.

ATTRACTIONS: Near Sutton, a few km off SH 87 is New Zealand's only natural salt lake and a rare skink has been discovered in the surrounding hills. Fascinating rock outcrops are scattered throughout the entire region which is dominated by the Rock and Pillar Range. Middlemarch is a sleepy little village and first settlement of any size since leave the Taieri Plains. The recently closed Otago Central Railway has been restored as a cyclists, trampers & horse trail stretching 150 km from Middlemarch to Clyde. The gravel surface has been improved recently, and isn't as rough.

A few km off SH 87 near Hyde is Macraes Flat, with an historic Stanley's Hotel and an open-cast gold mine where a mountain is being moved to reach the precious metal below. To commemorate the importance of gold to the region the Otago Goldfields Park protects a number of historical sites scattered throughout the region. Ranfurly with its broad streets is the main town of the Maniototo. Nearby Naseby is becoming a popular mountain biking area, see Options page 23.

OPTIONS: **ALTERNATIVE** MIDDLEMARCH - RANFURLY (62 km) on the vehicle-free OTAGO CENTRAL RAIL TRAIL as it passes through some spectacular scenery using bridges, viaducts, tunnels, cuttings, embankments, flocks of sheep and gates to open and shut. Some call it the Ale Trail due to the number of pubs on this part of the route.

The gravel surface has been improved recently. If it's too rough, SH 87 runs parallel to the trail. but you'll miss the specacular Upper Taieri Gorge and Tunnel. Obtain up-to-date information before using, DoC have produced an information sheet for users. Check with Alexandra Visitor Centre to see if they will hold your excess lugguage - send it from Dunedin by shuttle bus. Can be hot and dry in summer with little shade. If blowing, strong nor-westerly winds might pose a problem to Ranfurly. One way bike hire is possible from some Dunedin and Alexandra bike shops.

LINK ROAD KYEBURN (SH 87) - PALMERSTON (SH 1) on SH 85. 63 km.
This is called the Pigroot. A gradual climb from the Junction of SH 87 & 85 at Kyeburn for 15 km to the summit (640m) then roller-coasters for much of the 33 km to the Macraes Flat turn off.
PIGROOT STREAM: picnic area. DEAD HORSE PINCH: picnic area
Gradients ease from Macraes Flat turn off and a steady descent follows to
DUNBACK: Store. then almost flat for 13 km to PALMERSTON: See page 17 for onward travel.

5b RANFURLY - OMAKAU - CROMWELL (Queenstown). 173km

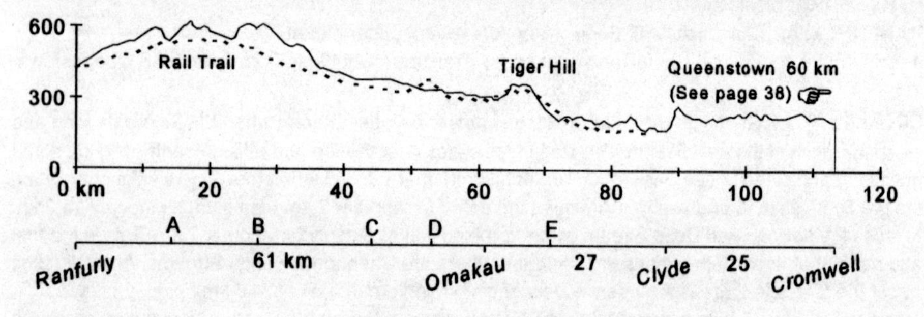

SERVICES: **RANFURLY:** See previous section. **A) WEDDERBURN:** Pub, bkpr hostel.
B) HILLS CREEK: picnic area. **C) BECKS:** Alt 380m hotel. **D) LAUDER:** Alt 350m. Store, pub.
OMAKAU: Alt 300m, pop 200. Store, motor camp, hotel. **OPHIR:** (2 km E of Omakau off SH 87) bkpr hostel (seasonal), pub. **E) CHATTO CREEK:** Alt 240m, pub.
ALEXANDRA: Alt 150m, pop 5,000. ***i:*** 22 Centennial Ave ☎448-9515.
Food: All outlets. Accom: 2 motor camp; 7 motel; hotel. Bicycle Shops.
CLYDE: Alt 170m. All types of food outlets except supermarket. Motor camp; motel 2; bkpr hostel.
LAKE DUNSTAN: picnic areas at Dairy Creek (also toilets), Champagne Creek & Jacksons.
CROMWELL: Alt 220m, pop 3,300. ***i:*** 47 The Mall ☎445-0212. Food: All outlets.
Accom: 4 motor camp (2 at Bannockburn); 6 motel; 2 hotel.
Transport: Bus & shuttles to/from Chch, Queenstown, Dunedin & Fox.
NOTE: See page 38 for travel to/from Queenstown or Chch and page 53 to/from the West Coast.

GRADIENTS: Easy terrain much of the way from Ranfurly except for moderate rolling hills between Wedderburn & St Bathan's turn-off, a 3 km beyond Hills Creek and a steep 1 km uphill and 4½ km quite steep descent at Tiger Hill between Omakau & Chatto Creek. Leave the rail trail at Chatto Creek if going direct to Cromwell.

At Clyde is a 1 km quite steep climb to join new Lake Dunstan. Going through Cylde and taking the dam road reduces the elevation gain. At the top long sweeping rolls skirt alongside the lake going all the way to Cromwell, the town centre is 1 km off SH 6 across the bridge.

ATTRACTIONS: The wide-open spaces and silence of the Maniototo Plains can be quite intimidating. It is hard to imagine in their hey-day a century ago, the quaintly named Naseby, St Bathans and other localities had several thousand inhabitants, also see Options below. Time seems to have stood still with many retaining the atmosphere of the pioneering days. The entire stretch of the Rail Trail now open some of it is rough. Interesting rocky outcrops continue to dot the route.

Clyde is a charming place despite the dam looming over it. The old Cromwell Gorge has now become the new Lake Dunstan. Filled in 1992, years late with huge cost over-runs this marvel of modern engineering seemed it would never be completed. Ponder as you pedal alongside the lake what might happen if the two fault lines the dam is built on suddenly move or the unstable hillsides slide into to lake.

OPTIONS: **ALTERNATIVE i** IDABURN - OMAKAU along the very quiet Ida Valley Road through... OTUREHUA (vintage store, pub, bkpr hostel;). POOLBURN (pub with bkpr accom) & OPHIR (seasonal bkpr hostel, pub). Mostly easy gradients except for one large hill between Poolburn and Ophir. Near Oturehua is the historic Hayes Engineering Works, where NZ's No: fencing wire was invented. Ophir also has a number of historic buildings the gold rush era.

ALTERNATIVE ii RANFURLY - OTUREHUA - OMAKAU - ALEXANDRA - CLYDE on the car-free OTAGO CENTRAL RAIL TRAIL. For Services see Alternative i above. This is a continuation of the 150 km rail corridor between Middlemarch and Clyde has been converted to a cycling, tramping and horse riding trail. See previous section's Options for Middlemarch - Ranfurly. Obtain up-to-date information before using, DoC have produced a brochure for users. If by-passing Alexandra, leave the rail trail and join SH 85 at Chatto Creek until Springvale, then go right to Clyde. The gravel surface has been improved recently but don't use overloaded bikes, send excess gear by shuttle to Alexandra. Check with the visitor centre to see if they will hold your stuff for a few days. If too rough, use SH 85 and Ida Valley Road, which run parallel to the trail for much of the way but you'll miss the specacular Poolburn Viaduct, Gorge and tunnels. One way bike hire is possible from some Dunedin and Alexandra bike shops.

SIDE TRIP 10 km W of SH 85 is ST BATHANS: Alt 580m, pop 50, hotel. All that remains of this once thriving mining town is the Vulcan Hotel, Post Office, Gold Office and hall.

The Blue Lake of St Bathans was formed by hydraulic elevating after miners turned a 120 metre high hill into a 70 metre deep hole. Mining only stopped when it threatened the main street with plenty of gold said to remain underwater. The Vulcan Hotel is reputed to be haunted.

LINK ROAD RANFURLY - DUNTROON much of it gravel. 14 km north of Ranfurly is . . .
NASEBY: Alt 600m, pop 130. Food: Dairy, pub. Accom: Motor camp; hotel 2 (also bkpr & motel accom). Naseby is another old gold mining town with period charm and a popular mountain biking area, especially in the nearby Naseby forest. The Royal Hotel has bike hire, a repair workshop and guiding.

17km after Naseby is KYEBURN (Historic hotel/restaurant). Then climb 22km to remote DANSEY'S PASS: motor camp (9km after the pass, 14 km before Duntroon). Isolated and narrow gravel track much of the way between the hotel and motor camp with some steep sections. See link road page 37 for onward travel.

CENTRAL

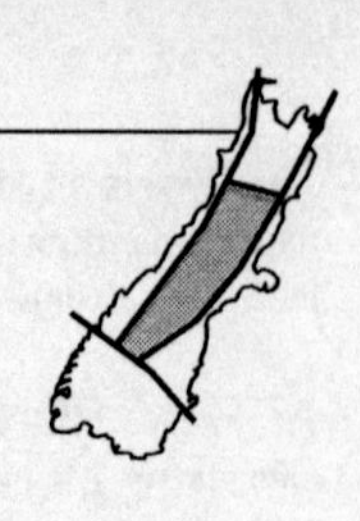

HIGHLIGHTS (not in any order of preference)

Christchurch City & Port Hills
Dunedin & Otago Peninsula
Whales & dolphins at Kaikoura
Marlborough Sounds Maritime Park
Penguins & Historic Precinct at Oamaru
North Canterbury coastal scenery
North Otago coastal scenery
Akaroa & Banks Peninsula
Otago Central Rail Trail &
Taieri Gorge Railway

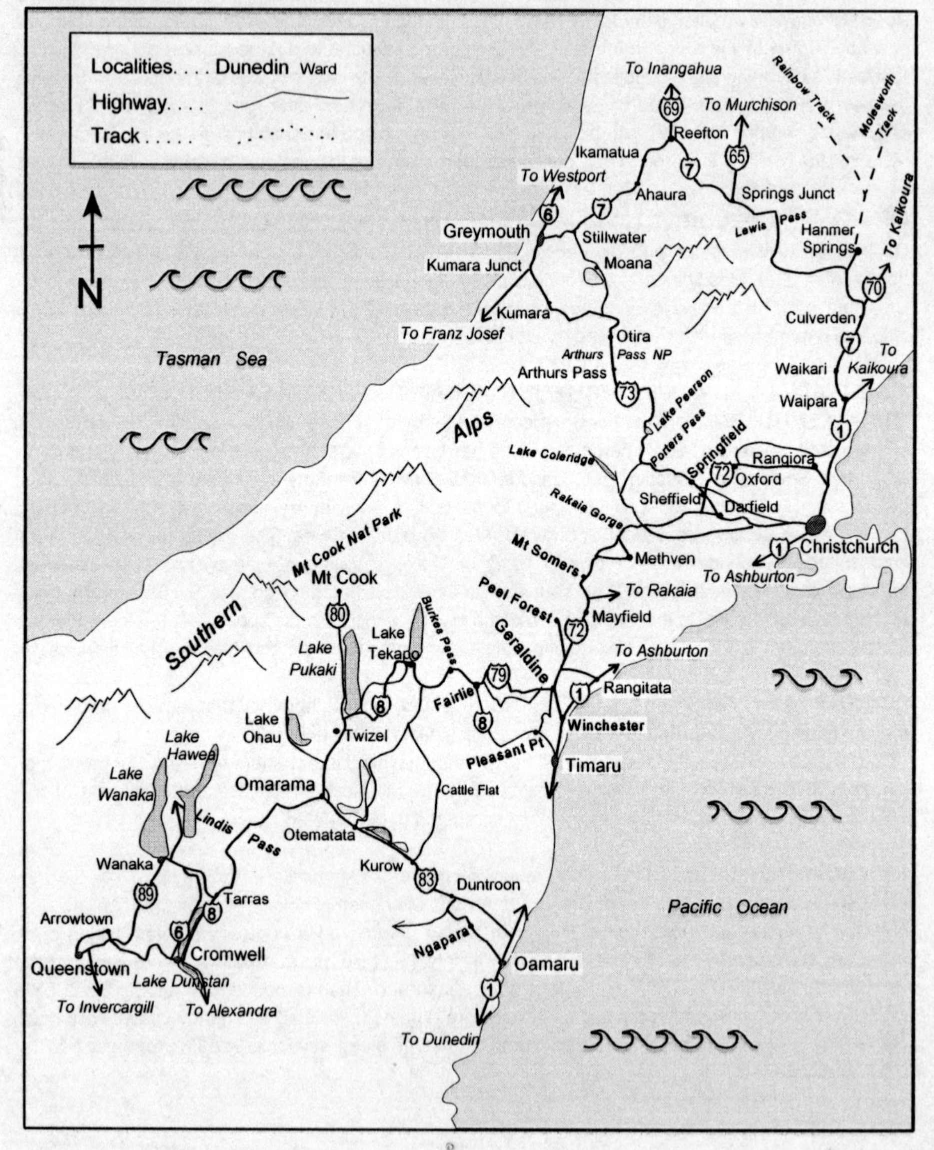

6 CHRISTCHURCH - LEWIS PASS - GREYMOUTH.

ROUTE:	SH1/7
6a) CHCH - LEWIS PASS	189 km
6b) LEWIS PASS - GREYMOUTH	143 km
Total	332 km

ALTERNATIVE 6b) REEFTON - GREYMOUTH. The easier SH 7 via Ngahere or the more hilly route passing Blackball. Both options separate at Ikamatua and meet at Greymouth. See page 29.

SIDE TRIP 6a) To HANMER SPRINGS.

6b) i HUKARERE - WAIUTA. ii NGAHERE - NELSON CREEK. (Both are partly gravel, page 29).

LINK ROAD 6a) i CULVERDEN - WAIAU - KAIKOURA on SH 70. See page 15.

ii HANMER SPRINGS (SH 7) - MOLESWORTH TRACK - SEDDON (SH 1). See page 27.

iii HANMER SPRINGS - RAINBOW TRACK - St ARNAUD (SH 63). See page 27.

6b) i SPRINGS JUNCTION - MURCHISON (SH 6) on SH 65. See page 64.

ii REEFTON (SH 7) - INANGAHUA JUNCTION(SH 6) on SH 69. See page 29.

iii STILLWATER (SH 7) - MOANA - JACKSONS (SH 73). See page 30.

6a CHRISTCHURCH - WAIPARA - LEWIS PASS. 189km

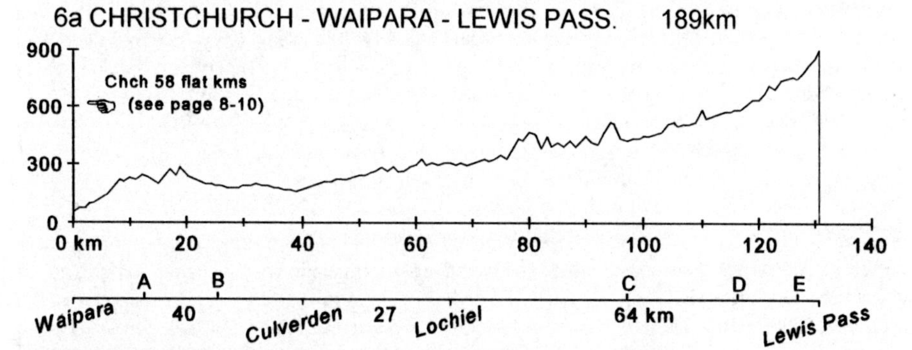

SERVICES: **CHRISTCHURCH:** See page 13 for travel to . . .

WAIPARA: Alt 60m, pop 270. Tearooms, restaurant, store, bkpr hostel, hotel.

A) WAIKARI: Alt 220m, pop 250. Tearooms, pub, domain camping. Inexpensive cyclists' homestay, (see below) for details. **B) HURUNUI:** Alt 190m. Hotel.

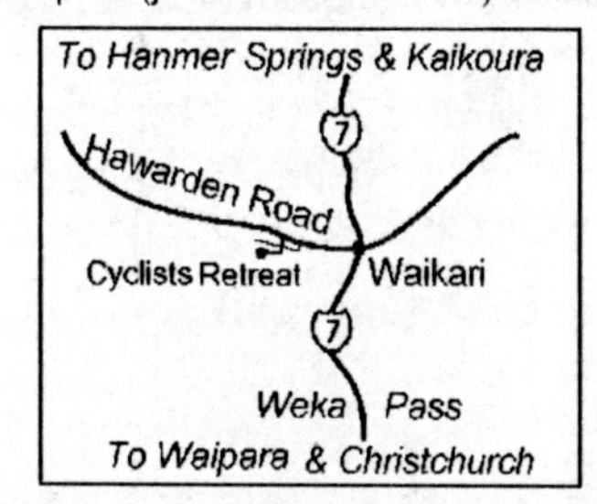

BALMORAL FOREST: DoC style camping (toilet, table, water).
CULVERDEN: Alt 175m, pop 400. Store, takeaways/tearooms, pub, motel.
LOCHIEL: (Hanmer Springs turn off) Alt 305m. refreshments at nearby Waiau Ferry Bridge.
HANMER SPRINGS: (10 km off SH 7) Alt 365m, pop 1300. ***i:*** DoC, Amuri Ave, ☎315-7128.
Food: All outlets except supermarket. Accom: 4 motor camp; hostel (2 bkpr, 1 YHA); 10 motel; 2 hotel. Transport: Shuttle to/from Chch. Bicycle Shop.
C) HOPE RIVER BRIDGE: Picnic area. **BOYLE SETTLEMENT:** Alt 580m, shelter.
D) SILVIA FLAT: Alt 590m, picnic area (table, sandflies) adjacent SH 7 & thermal pools in the river.
E) DEER VALLEY: DoC camping (toilet, water, table, sandflies) adj SH 7.
St JAMES WALKWAY: Alt 860m, DoC camping(toilet, table, shelter), 1 km E of . . .
LEWIS PASS: Altitude 905m, picnic area. No Sevices for 80 km between Hanmer & Maruia.

GRADIENTS: Mostly flat from Chch to Waipara, then join SH 7 and gradually climb to Weka Pass (247m). Rolls for 7 km through Waikari with two quite steep hills before Hurunui, after which the highway becomes almost flat, passing through Culverden to Red Post Corner (SH 70 junction). Continues similar for the next 25 km to Lochiel (Hanmer turn-off) except for a couple of minor hills near Brown's Stream.

Apart from a small drop soon after Lochiel, the terrain is mostly flat for the first 10 km. Then the gradients start to roll as SH 7 leaves the plains behind and enters the Waiau Valley. 10 km of hills follow as the road negotiates bluffs, dipping and climbing to cross side valleys. Though not very long some gradients are steep, climbing high above the valley floor, particularly between Handyside & Gorge Streams. A couple of steep hills follow, one between Glynne Wye and Hope River Bridge and another to cross Boyle Bluffs with the ups longer than the downs. After Boyle Settlement SH 7 undulates to Silvia Flat followed by a stepped climb for 14 km to reach Lewis Pass.

ATTRACTIONS: Weka Pass between Waipara & Waikari has a historic reserve and walkway containing Maori rock drawings, interesting limestone rock formations and a vintage railway. See the distinctive Frog Rock that looks amazingly like a goat or big pussy cat! Beyond Waikari go past the restored 1860's historic Hurunui Hotel, Balmoral Forest and small village of Culverden. At Lochiel, (Hanmer Springs turn-off) is the Waiau Ferry Bridge where bungy jumping and jet boating take place.

On an easy 10 km side trip off SH 7 is Hanmer Springs, a popular health resort with thermal hot pools. Mountain biking is becoming increasingly popular in and around Hanmer Forest, bike hire and servicing available. Also available are walking tracks, horse treks and skiing. Here is one end of both the Molesworth & Rainbow Tracks.

Further along SH 7 a tramping track goes from Windy Point to Lake Sumner Forest Park and over Harper Pass to Arthur's Pass, a well off the beaten tourist track kind of place. A few kilometres north of Boyle Settlement adjacent to the highway by the Lewis River are the undeveloped Silvia Flat hot pools, although sometimes they're only tepid. Boyle is one end of St James Walkway, a sub-alpine tramp of several days on the eastern side of Lewis Pass.

OPTIONS: **SIDE TRIP** 10 km off SH 7 is HANMER SPRINGS, the South Island's première thermal resort, see above for services and attractions.

LINK ROAD i CULVERDEN (SH 7) - WAIAU - KAIKOURA (SH 1) on SH 70. See page 14.

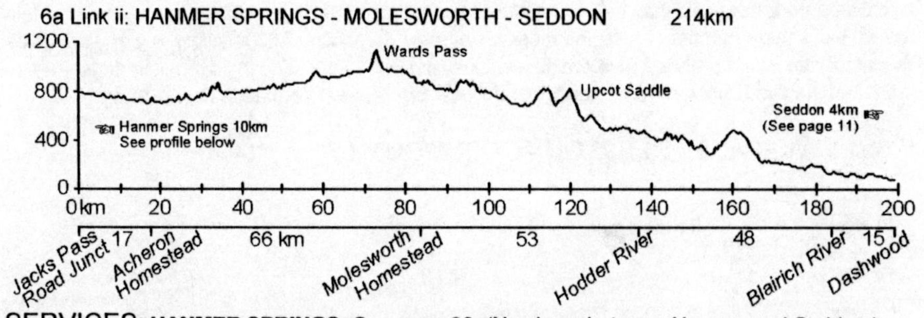

SERVICES: **HANMER SPRINGS:** See page 26. (No shops between Hanmer and Seddon.)
ACHERON HISTORIC HOMESTEAD: Alt 715m, DoC camping (toilets, water).
MOLESWORTH HISTORIC HOMESTEAD: Alt 870m, DoC camping (toilets, water).
HODDER RIVER: Alt 460m, Domain camping (toilet). **CAMDEN STATION:** Alt 405m, bkpr hostel.
BLAIRICH RIVER: Alt 125m, Domain camping (toilet). **SEDDON:** See page 11.

GRADIENTS & ATTRACTIONS: **The Molesworth Track is predominantly a rough gravel road passing through remote and isolated areas. It goes via the historic Acheron and Molesworth homesteads, ending at Dashwood, 5 km north of Seddon on SH 1. Managed by DoC, it is now open all year to cyclists, but permission from the station manager is required to use the road.**

Numerous hills, the most memorable comprise of 500m climb in 6km to Jacks Pass, 170m climb in 1½ km to Wards Pass and similar descent, and the 220m descent in 2½ km after Upcot Saddle. Care is required on this descent as it is steep with hairpin bends and loose gravel.

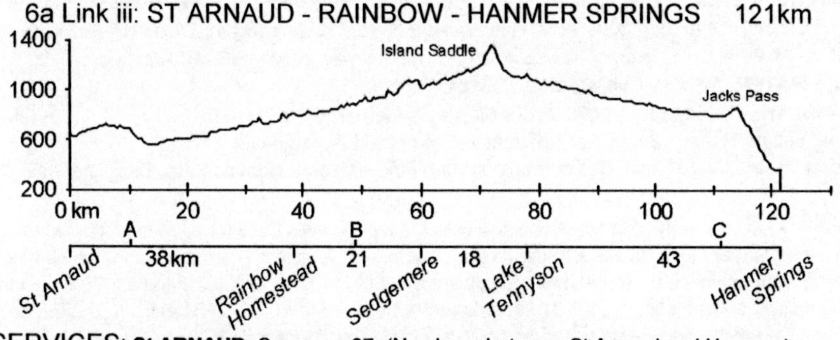

SERVICES: **St ARNAUD:** See page 67. (No shops between St Arnaud and Hanmer.)
A) SH63/RAINBOW JUNCT: Information display. **OLD RAINBOW HOMESTEAD:** Alt 800m, tollgate.
B) COLDWATER STREAM: Alt 890m, DoC camping (toilets, water).
LAKE SEDGEMERE: Alt 1020m, DoC hut & camping (toilets, water).
LONG GULLY: Alt 1130m, DoC hut (toilets, water) ½ km down side track.
LAKE TENNYSON: Alt 1120m, DoC camping (toilets, water) 1mile down side track.
C) JACKS PASS/RAINBOW JUNCT: Information display. **HANMER SPRINGS:** See page 26.

GRADIENTS & ATTRACTIONS: **This remote rough mostly gravel electricity pilon service road goes between St Arnaud and Hanmer Springs. It travels via Coldwater Stream, Island Saddle (1360m), Lake Tennyson, Clarence River and Jack's Pass. Bad corrugations much of the way but especially down Jack's Pass Road. The Rainbow Rage Rally in March is popular with mountain bikers.**

Scenically more enjoyable than the nearby Molesworth. Closed in winter. Not for the beginner or faint hearted! Not a huge number of hills, the most memorable comprise of 200m climb in 2km and similar descent to/from Island Saddle and 500m descent in 6km from Jacks Pass to Hanmer Springs. Pay the road toll at the Old Rainbow Homestead. Obtain local up-to-date information before using.

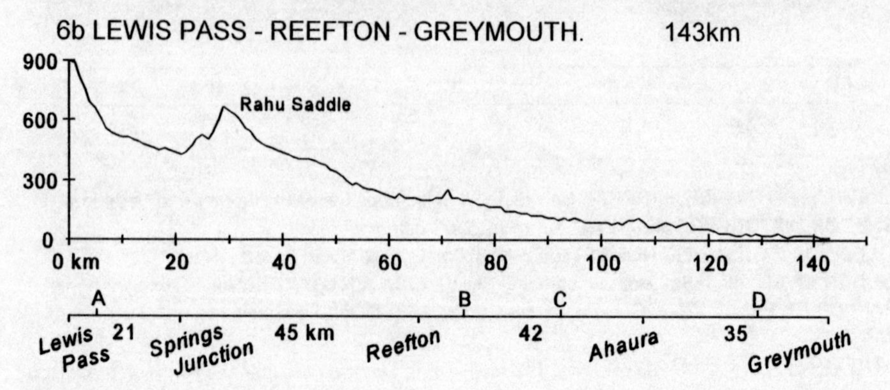

SERVICES: **LEWIS PASS:** Alt 905m, picnic area. No shops for 80 km between Hanmer and ...
A) MARUIA SPRINGS: Alt 605m. Hotel/restaurant/bkpr hostel (use of hot pools included in price).
MARBLE HILL: DoC camping (toilet, table) adj SH 7.
SPRINGS JUNCTION: Alt 430m, Tearooms/restaurant/motels.
REEFTON: Alt: 190m, pop 1,200. ***i:*** DoC, Broadway ☎732-8391. Food: All types of outlet except supermarket. Accom: Motor camp; bkpr hostel; 2 motel; hotel. Bicycle shop.
B) SLAB HUTT CREEK: DoC camping (toilet, table, water) gold panning. **MAWHERAITI:** Pub.
C) IKAMATUA: Alt 110, pop 200. Store. Hotel (also tent sites & bkpr accom). **TOTARA FLAT:** Pub.
AHAURA: Alt 90m. Store, pub, domain camping (toilet, shower, cabin). **NGAHERE:** pub.
D) STILLWATER: Alt 60m. Pub, store. **DOBSON:** Pub.
GREYMOUTH: Alt 10m, pop 13,000. ***i:*** Cnr Mackay & Herbert Sts ☎768-5101.
Food: All outlets. Accom: 2 motor camp; hostel (5 bkpr, 1 YHA); 16 motel; 8 hotel.
Transport: Train to/from Chch. Bus & shuttle to/from Fox, Nelson & Arthur's Pass. Bicycle shops.

GRADIENTS: A steady quite steep downhill from the top of Lewis Pass for 6 km to just past Maruia Springs, after that SH 7 tracks a mostly gentle down to Springs Junction. The climb begins immediately on leaving Springs Junction, sometimes steeply, for most of the 8 km to Rahu Saddle (670m). A long variable steep descent follows gradually easing as Reefton nears. A flattish 5 km from Reefton ends with a steep ½ km climb to Reefton Saddle and a similar ½ km descent on the other side. Becomes a gradual descent alongside Grey River to Greymouth, apart from a couple of smallish hills near Ahaura.

ATTRACTIONS: Lewis Pass National Reserve has extensive mountains, river flats and beech forest within its boundaries with plenty of walks along the way. Not far from the pass is Maruia Springs, one of only two commercial thermal hot springs resorts on the South Island. The (fairly expensive) complex features a Japanese style bathhouse. Marble Hill is a hill of marble, with a major fault line nearby and the start of the Lake Daniells Track.

After Springs Junction enter Victoria State Forest Park going over Rahu Saddle and into the Inangahua Valley. A few kilometres off SH 7 is Garvey Creek, a coal mine burning since 1951 and comes complete with smoke pouring from vents in the ground. Black's Point has a working gold stamping battery in the museum. Once called Quartzopolis, Reefton was one of NZ's richest gold producing regions and boasts having the world's first street lighting, is now yet another sleepy village.

The surrounding Victoria Forest Park has a number of gold mining relics and ghost towns, such as the side trip to Waiuta from just north of Ikamatua. A number of tramping tracks criss-cross the park, DoC has produced a useful brochure on the area. Gold panning without a licence is allowed in some places. Pass through several small communities between Reefton and Greymouth, the route is notable for the number of pubs.

Grey by name, grey by nature especially on cold wet days, Greymouth is the largest town on the West Coast. See the Great Wall of Greymouth, built to stop the Grey River from flooding the town centre and ruining shop keepers' merchandise. Point Elizabeth walkway and fossicking on the beach are other popular activities. The Brunner Mine a few kms north is the site of NZ's worst mining disaster in 1896.

OPTIONS: **LINK ROAD i** SPRINGS JUNCTION - MURCHISON on SH 65. See page 64.
LINK ROAD ii REEFTON - INANGAHUA JUNCTION is an easy 34 km descent on SH 69 alongside Inangahua River, INANGAHUA BRIDGE: bkpr hostel, for beyond Inangahua see page 63.

ALTERNATIVE IKAMATUA - GREYMOUTH along the sealed Atarau Rd on the west bank of the Grey River and skirting the eastern foothills of the Paparoa Mountains. More hilly but quieter than SH 7 which itself is deserted. A 1½ km detour from the road goes to famous . . .
BLACKBALL: Alt 150m, pop 350. Store, pub, salami factory, (Not the Blackball Hilton) bpkr hotel. Blackball is the eastern access point for the Croesus Track to Barrytown on the West Coast.
TAYLORVILLE: Store, pub. A bridge crosses the Grey River between Blackball & Stillwater.

SIDE TRIP i HUKARERE - WAIUTA Distance 13 km. Leave SH 7 about 4 km north of Ikatamua. Travel on a narrow road (gravel and winding uphill from Blackwater) to see the recently abandoned ghost town of WAIUTA (DoC hut, locked but key available from Reefton Information Centre). Gold mining relics abound with a number of information displays. Gain access to Waiuta to Big River Track from here.

SIDE TRIP ii NGAHERE - NELSON CREEK: Pub, store, DoC camping (toilet, table, water) also gold panning. This a small settlement 10 km E of SH 7. Access from here on a gravel road to the remote LAKE HOCHSTETTER (DoC camping).

7 GREYMOUTH - ARTHUR'S PASS - CHRISTCHURCH.

ROUTE:	SH 73
7a) GREYMOUTH - ARTHUR'S PASS	99 km*
7b) ARTHUR'S PASS - CHRISTCHURCH	154 km**
Total	253 km

* Add 4 km if going via Stilllwater & Moana. ** Add 31 km if going via Lake Coleridge & Glentunnel.

ALTERNATIVE 7a) GREYMOUTH - JACKSONS. The busier SH 6 & 73 via Kumara or the quiet, more interesting route via Stillwater and Moana. Both options meet near Jacksons.
7b) i LAKE LYNDON - LAKE COLERIDGE - GLENTUNNEL - DARFIELD. Partly gravel. This can be used as an alternative to the steep Porter's Pass between Arthur's Pass & Christchurch or a link for heading south via Rakaia Gorge.
ii SHEFFIELD - YALDHURST. The busier SH 73 via Darfield or quiet Old West Coast Road.
LINK ROAD 7a) DONEGALS - HOKITIKA on the rough Old Chch Highway, see page 60.
7b) SHEFFIELD (SH 73) - OXFORD - WOODEND (SH 1) on SH 72 north of Chch. See page 15.

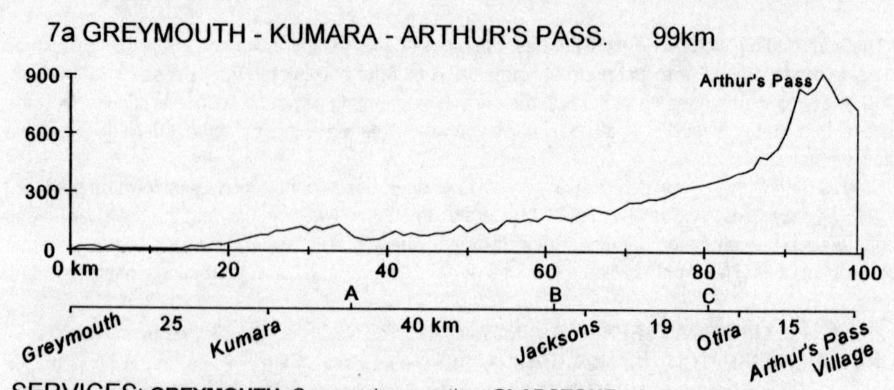

SERVICES: **GREYMOUTH:** See previous section. **GLADSTONE:** picnic area (table).
KUMARA JUNCTION: Seasonal bkpr hostel (also camp sites) in the old school.
KUMARA: Alt 65m, pop 370. Food: Dairy/takeaways, pub. Accom: Hotel, motel.
A) DONEGAL'S: picnic area. **B) THE AVENUE:** picnic area. **JACKSONS:** Pub; cabins.
C) KELLY'S CREEK: DoC camping (shelter, toilets, water) adj SH 73.
OTIRA: Alt 420m. Hotel/tearooms, bkpr hostel. **VIADUCT LOOKOUT:** picnic area.
ARTHUR'S PASS: Alt 920m, picnic area.
ARTHUR'S PASS VILLAGE: Alt 730m, pop 50. ***i:*** DoC, Main Rd ☎318-9211.
Food: Store, tearooms, restaurant. Accom: DoC camping at the picnic shelter opposite Park HQ (water, toilets, shelter); Hostel (1 bkpr, 1 YHA); motel. Transport: Train to/from Greymouth & Chch. Shuttles to/from Chch, Greymouth & Hokitika.

GRADIENTS: Easy terrain heading south on SH 6 to Kumara Junction, then go east towards Arthur's Pass on SH 73. Rolls and undulates through Kumara and after Dillmanstown join Taramakau River heading upstream past Moana turn off & Jacksons. Beyond Aickens join Otira River and begin to climb in earnest with the mountains closing in. 4 km past Otira enter the Otira Gorge climbing for 6 km, becoming very steep! A viaduct with a gentle 11.7% incline has been built to replace the even steeper zig zag. Associated nearby roadsworks have now finished. A final climb after the viaduct to the pass (920m) from where SH 73 rolls and winds mostly down for 4 km to Arthur's Pass Village.

ATTRACTIONS: Kumara is the site of the first gold rush on the West Coast, once having 46 hotels and nearby Dillmanstown another 12. Richard Seddon, a famous Prime Minister lived there for several years. A few scenic reserves dot the foothills and small settlements nestle in the shadow of the Southern Alps. At Jacksons is the last remaining of five coaching inns that catered to travellers before the railway. Arthur's Pass is one of the less glamorous and uncrowded national parks though no less spectacular. It is a trampers park with climbing, skiing, glow worming and bird spotting (especially keas).

OPTIONS: **ALTERNATIVE** GREYMOUTH - MOANA - JACKSONS. Head out of Greymouth towards Reefton on SH 7, go right (east) at . . . STILLWATER: (Pub, store), passing . . .
KAIMATA: DoC style camping (toilet, water, table) and
MOANA: Alt 90m, pop 100. Store/takeaways, motor camp, hotel (also cabins for cyclists).

The highway undulates gently most of the way with an occasional hill. Joins SH 73 near Jacksons. Moana nestles on the shores of Lake Brunner where, we are told "the fish die of old age". Other features include the Brunner Mine Historic Reserve, an interesting look at a bygone era and NZ's worst mining tragedy. Arnold River Power Station is down a short detour.

7b ARTHUR'S PASS - PORTER'S PASS - CHRISTCHURCH. 154km

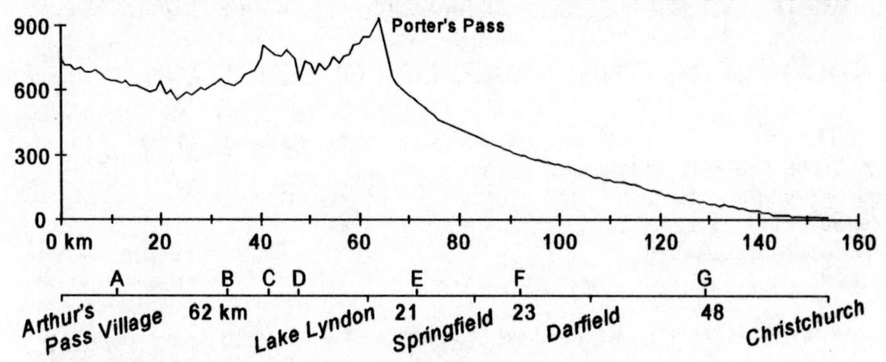

SERVICES: **ARTHUR'S PASS VILLAGE:** See previous section above.
GREYNEY'S FLAT: DoC camping (shelter, toilet, table, water) adjacent SH 73.
KLONDYKE CORNER: Alt 670m, DoC camping (shelter, toilet, table) adj SH 73.
A) BEALEY: Alt 635m, hotel. **B) LAKE PEARSON:** DoC camping (toilets) at west end of lake.
FLOCK HILL: Lodge (also bkpr accom and tent sites, but expect unhygenic conditions).
C) CRAIGIEBURN FOREST: DoC camping (shelter, toilet).
D) CAVE STREAM SCENIC RESERVE: picnic area (toilets). **PORTER'S RIVER:** picnic area.
LAKE LYNDON: Alt 850m, picnic area (shelter, table). **E) KOWHAI:** picnic area (table).
SPRINGFIELD: Alt 390m, pop 350. Store, tearooms. Domain camping (toilet, water, coin showers, no cabins); YHA hostel; hotel. **F) SHEFFIELD:** Alt 300m, Bakery, pub.
DARFIELD: Alt 200m. All types of food outlets except supermarket. Hotel, motel (incl bkpr accom).
KIRWEE: Pub, shop in petrol station. **G) WEST MELTON:** Pub, dairy. **YALDHURST:** Pub, takeaways.
CHRISTCHURCH: See pages 7-9.

GRADIENTS: On leaving Arthur's Pass SH 73 continues to roll down through the beech forest, emerging at Klondyke Corner where the Bealey and broad Waimakariri Rivers meet and surrounding mountains recede. Long easy gradients follow for much of the way to Lake Lyndon, interspersed by minor saddles or steep drops and climbs to cross streams.

An undulating climb from Lake Lyndon to Porter's Pass (945m) before a very steep 400m descent in 4 km, easing to a gradual decline into Springfield. Join the Canterbury Plains all the way into Chch, although barely noticeable the highway is tracking downhill. For directions into Chch (see pages 7-9).

ATTRACTIONS: Spectacular scenery continues after Arthur's Pass as beech forest gives way to open tussock country but still surrounded by high bare mountains. Craigieburn Forest Park, Cave Stream, Broken River, Kura Tauhiti Conservation Area (Castle Hill limestone outcrops), Lakes Grasmere, Pearson & Lyndon are some of the more interesting places on the highway. Several clubs have ski fields in the surrounding mountains. Descend Porter's Pass to join the Canterbury Plains.

OPTIONS: **ALTERNATIVE i** LAKE LYNDON - LAKE COLERIDGE - GLENTUNNEL - DARFIELD. Add 31 km if using this route instead of Porter's Pass. Although there are some hills, it avoids the steep Porter's Pass. A usually not too bad gravel road between LAKE LYNDON: picnic area (shelter, water, table) and LAKE COLERIDGE (B&B). Then sealed and rolling to SH 72, or go right (south) to Rakaia Gorge. see page 31. GLENTUNNEL: Dairy, pub, motor camp. & COALGATE: Pub, cabins.

ALTERNATIVE ii SHEFFIELD - YALDHURST on the quiet Old West Coast Road, mostly gentle downhill, no services. This is about 5 km shorter than SH 73.

8 CHCH - GERALDINE - OMARAMA - QUEENSTOWN.

ROUTE:

	Various	via Hororata	via Canal	SH 83
8a) CHRISTCHURCH - GERALDINE	172 km	169 km		
8b) GERALDINE - OMARAMA	178 km		175 km	
8c) OMARAMA - QUEENSTOWN	170 km			
link OMARAMA - OAMARU				118 km
Total	520 km			

ALTERNATIVE 8a) ALYESBURY CORNER - RAKAIA GORGE. SH 73/72 through Darfield or the easier, quieter route through Hororata. Beware fords in wet weather.
8b) i GERALDINE - FAIRLIE On SH 79 or a variety of side roads, some gravel.
ii LAKE TEKAPO - LAKE PUKAKI. SH 8 or the more interesting hydro canal road.
8c) ARROWTOWN - QUEENSTOWN On the quieter, longer Malaghan Road or SH 6.

SIDE TRIP 8a) i To METHVEN. ii ARUNDEL - PEEL FOREST.
8b) i LAKE TEKAPO - LAKE ALEXANDRINA, gravel road. ii To LAKE OHAU.
iii OMARAMA - CLAY CLIFFS, gravel road. iv To Mt COOK.
8c) i QUEENSTOWN - GLENORCHY. ii QUEENSTOWN - SKIPPERS CANYON.

LINK ROAD 8a) i MAYFIELD (SH 72) - RAKAIA TOWNSHIP (SH 1) on THOMPSON TRACK.
ii ORARI BRIDGE (SH 72) - RANGITATA (SH 1).
8b) i TIMARU (SH 1) - PLEASANT POINT - FAIRLIE on SH 8.
See page 16 for the above link roads.
ii OMARAMA (SH 8) - OAMARU (SH 1) on SH 83.
8c) TARRAS (SH 8) - WANAKA (SH 6) on SH 8a.

8a CHRISTCHURCH - RAKAIA GORGE - GERALDINE. 172km

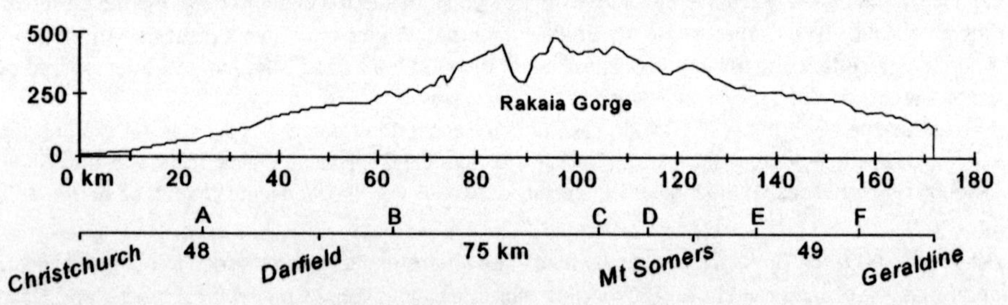

SERVICES: **CHRISTCHURCH:** See pages 7-9).
YALDHURST: Pub, takeaways. **A) WEST MELTON:** Pub, dairy. **KIRWEE:** Pub.
DARFIELD: Alt 200m. All types of food outlets except supermarket. Hotel, motel (incl bkpr accom).
COALGATE: Pub, cabins. **B) GLENTUNNEL:** Alt 230m. Dairy, pub, motor camp.
RAKAIA GORGE: Alt 275m. Domain camping (toilets, water, table); lodge (expensive).

C) PUDDING HILL: Chalets (3 km off SH 72/77). **ALFORD FOREST:** Alt 425m. Picnic area (toilets, tables, moas). **TAYLOR'S STREAM** picnic area (toilet, tables).
D) STAVELY: Alt 360m. Store, picnic area. **BOWYER STREAM:** picnic area.
Mt SOMERS: Alt 360m, pop 290. Store, restaurant, pub. Motor camp; Domain camping (toilet, water, table, coin showers); motel. **E) MAYFIELD:** Alt 260m, pop 200. Store/tearooms, pub.
F) ARUNDEL: Alt 200m, picnic area (toilets, table) adjacent SH 72 & Rangitata River.
GERALDINE: Altitude 120m, population 2,100. ***i:*** Talbot St ☎693-8597. Food: All outlets.
Accom: 2 motor camp, (1 is 7 km E of Geraldine); 3 motel; bkpr hostel; hotel. Bicycle Shop.
Transport: Bus & shuttles to/from Chch, Queenstown & Timaru.

GRADIENTS: Gentle climb out of Chch across Canterbury Plains. At Darfield go left (west) joining SH 72 at Homebush, remaining fairly flattish until Glentunnel then rolling hills to Windwhistle. At Rakaia Gorge the highway suddenly plunges 200m in 2 km from the upper terrace before levelling out for a short distance to the bridge. A steep climb begins immediately after crossing the river, gradually easing but becoming steeper again as the top nears at the Methven turn-off. Easy gradients follow, mostly gentle down all the way to Geraldine as the highway skirts the foothills of the eastern ranges.

ATTRACTIONS: Mostly standard farming country while on the Canterbury Plains, the exception being the impressive Rakaia Gorge, the river is popular for fishing and jetboating. After the Gorge, several scenic reserves dot the foothills of the eastern ranges, such as Mt Somers, Peel Forest, Orari & Waihi Gorges, all are a few kilometres off SH 72. They contain walkways of variable length and remnants of native bush that once covered much of the area. Other activities the area offers are skiing at Mt Hutt, hot air ballooning from Methven, parachuting from Pudding Hill, Moa spotting at Alford Forest and rafting the Rangitata. Geraldine is one of NZ's more pleasant towns, servicing rural communities and has a country music festival in summer, a vintage car museum and nearby Talbot Forest.

OPTIONS: **ALTERNATIVE** ALYESBURY CORNER - HORORATA - RAKAIA GORGE.
This is 3 km shorter than through Darfield. At Aylesbury Corner leave SH 73, cross railway tracks to HORORATA: Alt 190m, pub. Several km before Hororata, two normally dry fords may have water flowing in them if there has been recent prolonged heavy rain. At Hororata take first exit at the round-about to Rakaia Gorge. The highway rises all the way but is barely discernible until after Hororata.

SIDE TRIP i 5 km south of Rakaia Gorge and then 14 km off SH 72 (there is an access road to the north and south of the town) is the typically rural town of . . .
METHVEN: Alt 310m, pop 1,000. Food: All outlets except supermarket.
Accom: Motor camp; 2 bkpr hostel; 3 motel; hotel. Transport: Bus to/from Chch & Qutn.
It comes alive in winter with skiers & snowboarders using the nearby Mt Hutt.

SIDE TRIP ii ARUNDEL - PEEL FOREST: Store, DoC motor camp (kitchen, showers and now has cabins). Set in one of the last remnants of native bush found on the eastern foothills. Nearby are...
ORARI GORGE: DoC camping (toilet, table) & WAIHI GORGE: DoC camping (toilet, table).

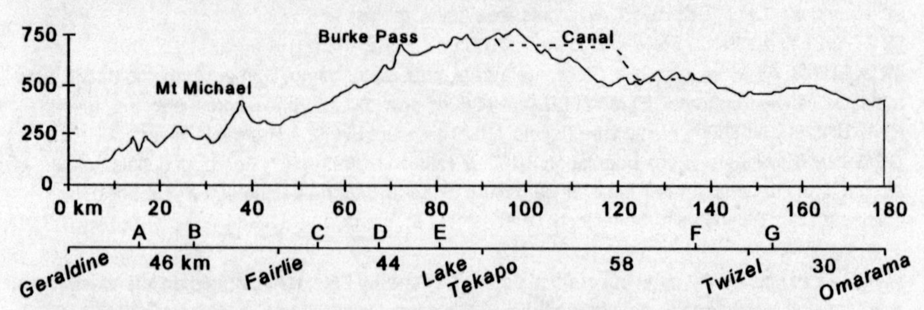

SERVICES: **GERALDINE:** See previous section. **A) HAPPY VALLEY:** picnic area.
B) OPUHA RIVER: Alt 235m. Domain camping at Skipton Bridge is closed due to flooding.
ALLANDALE: Alt 420m. Tearooms farm barn has re-opened (at the top of Mt Michael).
FAIRLIE: Alt 305m, pop 800. Food: All outlets except supermarket. Accom: Motor camp; bkpr hostel (closed for summer); 3 motel; 2 hotel. **C) KIMBELL:** Alt 390m. Pub, motel.
D) BURKE PASS VILLAGE: Alt 550m, pop 50. Store/tearooms/motel (closed Mondays?).
BURKE PASS: Alt 709m, picnic area. **DOG KENNEL CORNER:** picnic area.
E) EDWARD STREAM: picnic area.
LAKE TEKAPO: Alt 715m, pop 340. Food: All outlets except supermarket.
Accom: Motor camp (also motels); hostel (2 bkpr, 1 YHA); 2 motel; 2 hotel.
F) LAKE PUKAKI: Alt 545m, ***i:*** Mt Cook Lookout ☎435-3280 (shelter, toilets). Domain camping (toilet, water, table), 1 km E of Mt Cook turn-off. **LAKE WARDEL:** picnic area 1 km S of Mt Cook turn off.
TWIZEL: Alt 470m, pop 1200. ***i:*** Market Sq ☎435-3124. Food: All outlets except supermarket.
Accom: Motor camp; motel (incl bkpr accom); hotel; lodge (incl bkpr accom).
G) LAKE RUATANIWHA: picnic areas. **AHURIRI RIVER:** picnic area, 3 km N of . . .
OMARAMA: Alt 430m, pop 300. Food: Store, tearooms, takeaways. Accom: 2 motor camp (one 7 km E of Omarama on SH 83); 2 bkpr hostel (1 is 8 km N); motel; 3 hotel.
Transport: Bus & shuttles to/from Queenstown & Chch. Thrice weekly Mt Cook Connections summer shuttle to Oamaru gives 10% off transportation with this book.

GRADIENTS: Mornings between Geraldine and Tekapo can resemble rush hour in downtown Taipei as hordes of large buses trundle along the Blue Ribbon Route from Chch to Queenstown carrying the next wave of snoozing, jet lagged, packaged, processed tourists on their annual 7 day whistle stop holiday of a life time. See a possible alternative below. Things improve after lunch.

As the Canterbury Plains are left behind the low hills close in and terrain becomes hilly SH 79 undulates and rolls much of the way to Fairlie with a couple of long gradual climbs and steep descents at Gapes Valley and then through Pusey Gorge to Mt Michael.

On leaving Fairlie SH 8 starts with a gentle ascent that becomes undulating as Burke Pass Village nears. At the village, a steady, fairly steep climb starts, dips then climbs again becoming steep for the last 1 km to the pass (709m). A gentle descent into the MacKenzie Basin where gradients undulate, apart from an occasional steeper up and down. Try the canal (see Options).

SH 8 continues in a similar fashion between Lakes Tekapo and Pukaki with some fairly long gradual up and downs. At Lake Pukaki the highway rolls along the lakeshore for several kms. On passing the Mt Cook turn-off the road descends fairly steeply, easing to almost flat into Twizel. A similar, almost flat continues past Lake Ruataniwha to Omarama. Note: strong north westerly winds blow periodically.

ATTRACTIONS: Try some of Barker's famous fruit wines in Geraldine. Mostly pastoral scenery on the way to another pleasant rural service town of Fairlie, with spectacular views from Mt Michael. Near Fairlie is the interesting Opihi Gorge. At the top of Burkes Pass the scenery changes dramatically on entering the high country tussock grasslands of the MacKenzie Basin with majestic mountains of the Southern Alps as a backdrop. MacKenzie Country is named after an alleged sheep rustler who last century is credited with its discovery. In spring ride along the avenue of multi-coloured lupins.

Lake Tekapo often has an incredible azure blue colour caused by rock flour suspended in the water that contrasts with the surrounding stark brown landscape. Climb Mt John for spectacular views and in 1970 recorded NZ's strongest winds at 250km/h. Also on My John is a observatory cafe with a telescope and amazing photos of outer space.

One of NZ's best scenic flights round Mt Cook depart from here. Tekapo is the highest point of the Waitaki Hydro Power Scheme and with Pukaki holds 26% of NZ's storage water for generating hydro-electricity. Try the flat canal road linking Tekapo with Pukaki; another glacier fed lake with Mt Cook as a backdrop. Twizel has heli-biking, rowing regattas on Lake Ruataniwha and a special breeding centre for black stilts, one of the world's rarest birds. Omarama is a popular gliding area and has interesting clay cliffs "Badlands" nearby.

OPTIONS: **ALTERNATIVE i** GERALDINE - FAIRLIE. There are a couple of quiet alternatives to sharing SH 79 with moronic bus drivers. The following is all sealed, the easiest and flatest but 23 km more than SH 79. Turn left 4½ km out of Geraldine off SH 79 and onto Earl Road. After 6 km go right on Goodwin Rd then bear left and over 7 moderate rolls of Seven Sisters Road. Go right at the T junction onto Waitohi Rd to Pleasant Point. A 5 km side trip on Upper Waitohi Rd goes to a memorial to Richard Pearse, who in 1903 may have beaten the Wright Brothers as first to achieve powered (but not controlled) flight. Go right at Pleasant Point on SH 8 to Fairlie.
PLEASANT POINT: Alt 65m, pop 1,000. All types of food outlets. Motor camp (Labour W/E to Easter). Then a barely noticeable climb, passing small settlements such as . . .
CAVE: Alt 155m, pop 100. Store, pub. Maori rock drawings nearby. ALBURY: Alt 225m, pop 80, pub.

Another option for the more adventurous is a quite complicated, sometimes gravel and more hilly route. It's about 13 km longer than SH 79. It is recommended to use a local map for this and the previous alternative, available from the visitor centre.

5km out of Geraldine bear left off SH 79 at Brenton Rd going through Hilton then Kakahu, at which a short detour goes to an historic lime kiln. After Kakahu all roads (some gravel) lead to Opihi River and HANGING ROCK BRIDGE (informal camping). After crossing Opihi River go first right on Gay's Pass Rd, right to Raincliff (surrounded by limestone cliffs), then left at the scout camp on the aptly named Spur Road. Spur Road becomes gravel as it starts to climb, up in steps, rolling at the top and a 3 km steep descent, offers stunning views of the surrounding area but is exposed so not recommended in bad weather. Rejoin SH 79 at Tondros Road, 5 km before Fairlie. Confused?

A 5 km detour from Raincliff on Middle Valley Road is PIONEER PARK: DoC camping (water, tables, shelter). Continuing along Middle Valley Road can be used instead of Spur Road to rejoin SH 79, about 7 km from Fairlie. This Middle Valley Road way is 14 km longer than SH 79.

ALTERNATIVE ii LAKE TEKAPO - HYDRO CANAL - LAKE PUKAKI.
Take first left 2 km out of Tekapo following "bullock trail" sign and another 2 km brings you to the canal. Cross the bridge and go downstream (right), SH 8 crosses the canal road about half way. Continues flat until a steep downhill to Lake Pukaki. At the bottom go left following the lake shore until joining SH 8. Total distance is 2½ km shorter than by SH 8. Take care when strong north westerlies blow.

SIDE TRIP i LAKE TEKAPO - LAKE ALEXANDRINA: Domain camping (water, toilet)approx 10km. Has a wildlife refuge for bird spotters and is popular for fishing. A get away from it all place.

SIDE TRIP ii between Twizel & Omarama to LAKE MIDDLETON: Domain camping (toilet, table, water) & LAKE OHAU: Lodge (also bunkhouse, no kitchen, 10 km off SH 8), motel (32 km from SH 8). TEMPLE FOREST: DoC huts and camping (toilet, water, table).

SIDE TRIP iii CLAY CLIFFS of Omarama. Commonly called "badlands" the elements have sculptured interesting rock formations. Access along a rough track a few km before Omarama. They're also visible to the right on the way to Lindis Pass.

LINK ROAD i FAIRLIE - TIMARU on SH 8. See page 16.

8b SIDE TRIP IV: MT COOK. 56km

PUKAKI CORNER - GLENTANNER 33 km GLENTANNER - MT COOK 23 km

SERVICES: **LAKE PUKAKI:** See above. **GLENTANNER:** Restaurant/tearooms/motor camp.
Mt COOK: Alt 745m, pop 200. ***i:*** DoC, Bowen Dr ☎435-1818.
Food: Tearooms (also very expensive and limited food supplies), takeaways, restaurant.
Accom: DoC camping (toilet, table, water, shelter) 3 km from village; Hooker & Mueller Huts (3 - 4 hour walk); Bkpr & YHA hostel; Hotel/motel/chalets. Transport: Bus to/from Chch & Queenstown daily. The Mt Cook Connections summer shuttle to/from Oamaru & Timaru (3 per week) gives 10% off transportation with this book.

GRADIENTS: At Pukaki Corner join SH 80 to Mt Cook as it undulates and gently rolls alongside Lake Pukaki with distant Southern Alps slowly looming closer. Elevation gain is only about 190m in 56 km. The only climbs of any length are to go a short way into side valleys to cross a couple streams near Glentanner. Mt Cook is in a cul-de-sac, so enjoy the periodic, ferocious north westerly tail winds on the way back down the valley, one person reports gently pedalling the 56 km in 1 hour 40 minutes!

ATTRACTIONS: Spectacular views unfold all the way up the valley from Pukaki Corner. Mt Cook National Park has within its boundaries almost all of Australasia's 3,000m mountains, making it a natural centre for climbers. Tramping and scenic flights are favoured pastimes in this majestic environment. Tramping possibilities include to Mueller Hut, Tasman Valley up Ball Road, Red Lakes & Mt Sebastopol and Hooker Glacier to Hooker Hut, although the latter is becoming more dangerous due to the slumping of the lateral moraine. This is an alpine environment so take care if venturing beyond the village.

The Tasman Glacier is NZ's longest and resembles a huge gravel pit. Hard to imagine only 14,000 years ago during the last great ice age it reached to the bottom end of Lake Pukaki with ice 600m deep at the Hermitage. Mt Cook recently lost more than 50m³ million of rock and ice in a huge avalanche, reducing its height by 10 metres. The village doesn't suffer the excesses of Queenstown with controlled development requiring buildings to blend with the environment. Sir Edmund Hillary trained here for the first successful attempt on Mt Everest. Being a long way from civilisation, food is expensive & limited.

8b LINK ROAD ii: OMARAMA - KUROW - OAMARU. 118km

ROUTE: OMARAMA - OAMARU on SH 83/1. add 4 km if going via Ngapara.

ALTERNATIVE DUNTROON - OAMARU. The busier, easier SH 83 & 1 via Pukeuri or the quieter, hilly, more interesting route through Ngapara.

LINK ROAD DUNTROON - DANSEY'S PASS - RANFURLY See page 23.

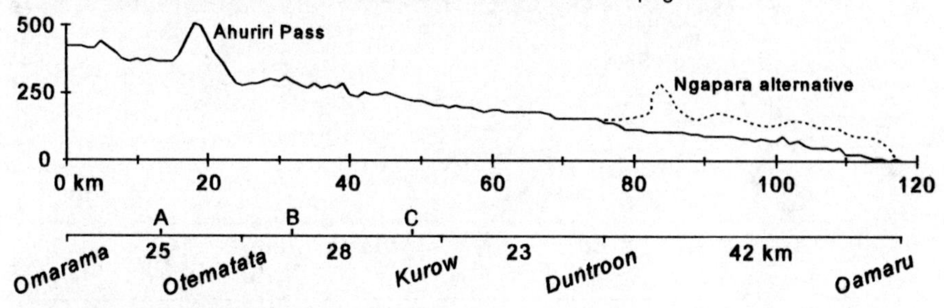

SERVICES: **OMARAMA:** See Section 8b above.

A) SAILOR'S CUTTING: Alt 425m. Domain camping (toilet, table, water) adjacent SH 83.

OTEMATATA: Alt 300m. Store, pub, motor camp, (also bkpr hostel & shop); hotel.

B) PARSON'S ROCK: Domain camping (toilets, table) adj SH 83.

LAKE WAITAKI: Domain camping (toilets, table) adj SH 83. **C) AWAKINO RIVER:** picnic area.

KUROW: Alt 210m, pop 580. ***i:*** Main Road ☎436-0812. Food: All outlets except supermarket. Accom: Motor camp; seasonal bkpr farm hostel (13 km S); motel; 3 hotel.

DUNTROON: Alt: 175m, pop 130. Tearooms, domain camping (showers, kitchen, cheap cabins); hotel.

OAMARU: See page 17.

GRADIENTS: Easy rolling country until after Sailor's Cutting then a fairly steep climb for 2 km to the Ahuriri Pass (505m) before a 3 km gradual descent to Otematata. SH 83 then undulates gently down to Kurow, thereafter hardly a hill to speak of as the road travels gently down to Oamaru. Try the Ngapara alternative from Duntroon, see options below.

ATTRACTIONS: Pass the man made Lakes Benmore, Aviemore & Waitaki, of the Waitaki Hydro Power project. Lake Waitaki was the last hand made dam using just pick and shovel. NZ's social welfare system has its roots at the deserted Waitaki Village. The Waitaki River is renowned for salmon. North westerly winds can be wonderful tail winds going down this stretch of highway but sometimes sea breezes blowing the other way reach Duntroon.

Maori rocks drawings can be seen adjacent SH 83, 3½ km before Duntroon. Duntroon is an important geological area with several distinctive natural features. These include Earthquakes, Elephant Rocks and the newly developed "Vanished World Fossil Trail". Another interesting feature are rattling rocks - a small stone within a stone that rattles when shaken - it's true! They're found near Earthquakes on Maerewhenua River but hard to find. Try the interesting alternative Ngapara route to Oamaru below.

OPTIONS: **ALTERNATIVE** DUNTROON - NGAPARA - OAMARU passing Elephant Rocks and NGAPARA with its impressive warehouse, ENFIELD: (pub) and WESTON (dairy) and where the famous Oamaru stone is quarried. This route is quite hilly around Elephant Rocks, before Ngapara, is 4 km longer, but more interesting and avoids the busy SH 1.

LINK ROAD DUNTROON - RANFURLY, much of it is gravel and some steep, over the remote . . .
DANSEY'S PASS: Motor camp, 14 km from Duntroon before the pass; historic hotel//restaurant after.
NASEBY: Alt 600m, pop 130. Dairy, pub. Motor camp; hotel (also bkpr & motel accom). Naseby is another old gold mining town with period charm, "2,000 ft above worry level" and becoming a popular mountain biking area, 14 km before RANFURLY: See page 21 & 23.

8c OMARAMA - CROMWELL - QUEENSTOWN. 170km

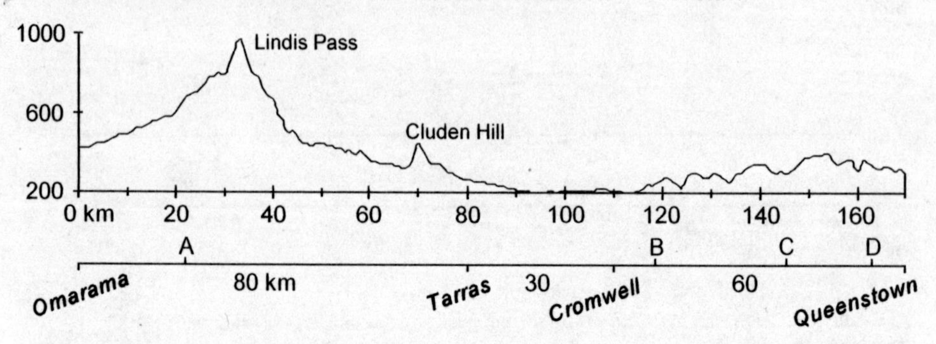

SERVICES: **OMARAMA:** see previous section (No services for 80 km betwen Omarama & Tarras).
A) DALRACNEY CREEK: Alt 630m, picnic area. **LINDIS PASS:** Alt 970m, picnic area.
TARRAS: Store, tearooms. Camping at the school is no longer permitted. Bkpr hostel, 4 km W of the village. **LAKE DUNSTAN:** picnic areas with tables adjacent to the lake at Bendigo (also toilets), Crippletown, Lions, Devil's and John Bulls Creek.
CROMWELL: Alt 220m, pop 3,300. ***i:*** 47 The Mall ☎445-0212. Food: All outlets.
Accom: 4 motor camp (2 at Bannockburn); 6 motel; 2 hotel.
Transport: Bus & shuttles to/from Chch, Queenstown, Dunedin & Fox.
B) KAWARAU GORGE: Mining centre, tearooms. **CAMP CREEK:** picnic area.
C) KAWARAU BRIDGE: bungy jumping, toilets. **LAKE HAYES:** Alt 320m, picnic area, motel.
D) FRANKTON: Alt 314m, pop 1,000.Food: All outlets. Accom: motor camp, hotel.
QUEENSTOWN: Alt 310m, pop 5,000. ***i:*** 1) Cnr Shotover & Camp St ☎442-4100 for tours.
2) DoC, 37 Shotover St ☎442-7933 for track information. Food: All outlets.
Accom: Motor camp 4; hostel (13 bkpr, 1 YHA); motel lots; hotel many. Bicycle shop.
Transport: Bus & shuttles to/from Chch, Invercargill, Milford Sound, Fox & Dunedin.

GRADIENTS: SH 8 climbs gently from Omarama with the surrounding hills slowly closing in. The gradients become more noticeable from Dalracney for the long 10 km gradual climb to Lindis Pass (970m) with the last 2 km becoming steep. After the Pass the road drops steeply at first, then rolls mostly down for 11 km. Gradients ease at Forest Hills Station then gently descends alongside the Lindis River but becomes fairly steep through two narrow Gorges. There's a 2 km variable steep climb beings on leaving the river to negotiate Cluden Hill (460m), then a 3 km quite steep descent before resuming the gentle downhill again for the last bit to Tarras.

At Lindis Crossing the highway starts to roll gently as it skirts new Lake Dunstan to Cromwell. On leaving Cromwell, the highway begins flattish before heading up-river into the narrow steep-sided Kawarau Gorge. Moderately steep up most of the way with an occasional down until Kawarau Bridge.

Fairly gentle rolls and undulations from there all the way to Frankton except for a moderate climb and short downhill at Lake Hayes and dip to cross the Shotover River. After Frankton the road undulates beside Lake Wakatipu, run the gauntlet of the urban traffic into Queenstown. Try the quieter Arrowtown alternative, see alternative below and page 54.

ATTRACTIONS: Near Omarama are the Clay Cliffs, an outcrop of unusual rock formations sculptured by the elements. See them to the right on the way to the Lindis Pass, a region of stark beauty and remote sheep stations. Just after Tarras is a track going up to Bendigo a ghost town from the gold rush era, shortly before new Lake Dunstan.Here also is Bendigo Station, home of the world famous Shrek the shy unshorn, shaggy sheep, rumour has it he was hiding from the farmer! Anyway, at Cromwell nibble on the giant fruit at the entrance to the town. Cromwell has been transformed from a tatty backwater into a lake side resort and fruit growing region of repute. It looks out of place somehow.

Travel through the stark spectacular Kawarau Gorge passing old gold mining sites, a bungy jumping bridge for those people with a deprived childhood, vineyards and pretty Lake Hayes before arriving at Queenstown. The undisputed tourist mecca of NZ, this town has a mind boggling array of activities to blow your budget on and locals expert at helping. One has to wonder at the mess they have made to the town, perhaps they didn't want to detract from the surrounding beauty. Central Otago can be hot and dry in summer and very cold in winter (they put the beer in the fridge to stop it freezing!).

OPTIONS: **ALTERNATIVE** ARROWTOWN - QUEENSTOWN on the quieter, longer and not too difficult Malaghan Road. Turn off SH 6 just after the Crown Range Road going through...
ARROWTOWN: Alt 420m, pop 1,100. Food: All outlets except supermarket.
Accom: Motor camp; 2 bkpr hostel; 4 motel; hotel.
ARTHUR'S POINT: Motor camp; hotel. QUEENSTOWN: See previous page.

SIDE TRIP i QUEENSTOWN - Mt ASPIRING National Park. This park borders Fiordland National Park and has more of the same spectacular scenery (less the fiords). Several tramping tracks traverse area including Routeburn and Milford. If these appear expensive and restrictive, then try others such as Greenstone/Caples or Rees/Dart Tracks. The base for exploring the many tramping tracks and last stop for supplies before heading into the mountains is . . .
GLENORCHY: ***i:*** DoC, Main Rd ☎442-9937. Takeaways, tearooms, restaurant. Motor camp (also small expensive shop), hotel. Shuttle to/from Queenstown and the tracks during the tramping season.

Travel west alongside Lake Wakatipu on a no exit road for 47 km with the lake and distant mountains always visible. The highway is now sealed all the way to Glenorchy. Undulates and steep rolls much of the way such as at 12 mile & Bennett's Bluffs. Can be busy in summer.

SIDE TRIP ii QUEENSTOWN - SKIPPER'S CANYON. Part way up Coronet Peak Road a narrow tortuous gravel road branches off to go to Skipper's Canyon. Once an important gold mining area it was one of the richest fields in the country. Very spectacular scenery but dangerous road. Four wheel drive tours, white water rafting and helicopter rides are other activities.

LINK ROAD TARRAS (SH 8) - WANAKA on SH 8a. Easy gradients at first then becomes rolling with some longer, steeper sections. No services. Can be used as part of an alternative to Queenstown going over the Crown Range, see pages 53-54 for onward travel.

SOUTH

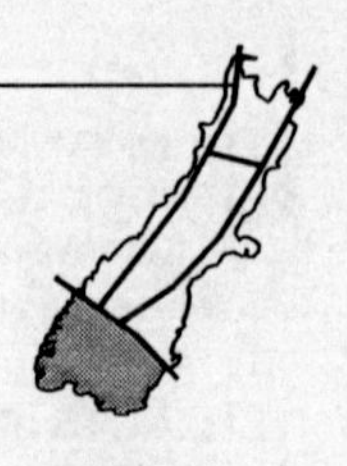

HIGHLIGHTS (not in any order of preference):

Queenstown
Fiordland National Park
Mt Aspiring National Park
Stewart Island National Park
Catlins Forest Park
Southern Scenic Route
Curio & Porpoise Bays
Clutha Valley
Gore's big fish?
Lake Waihola & Sinclair Wetlands

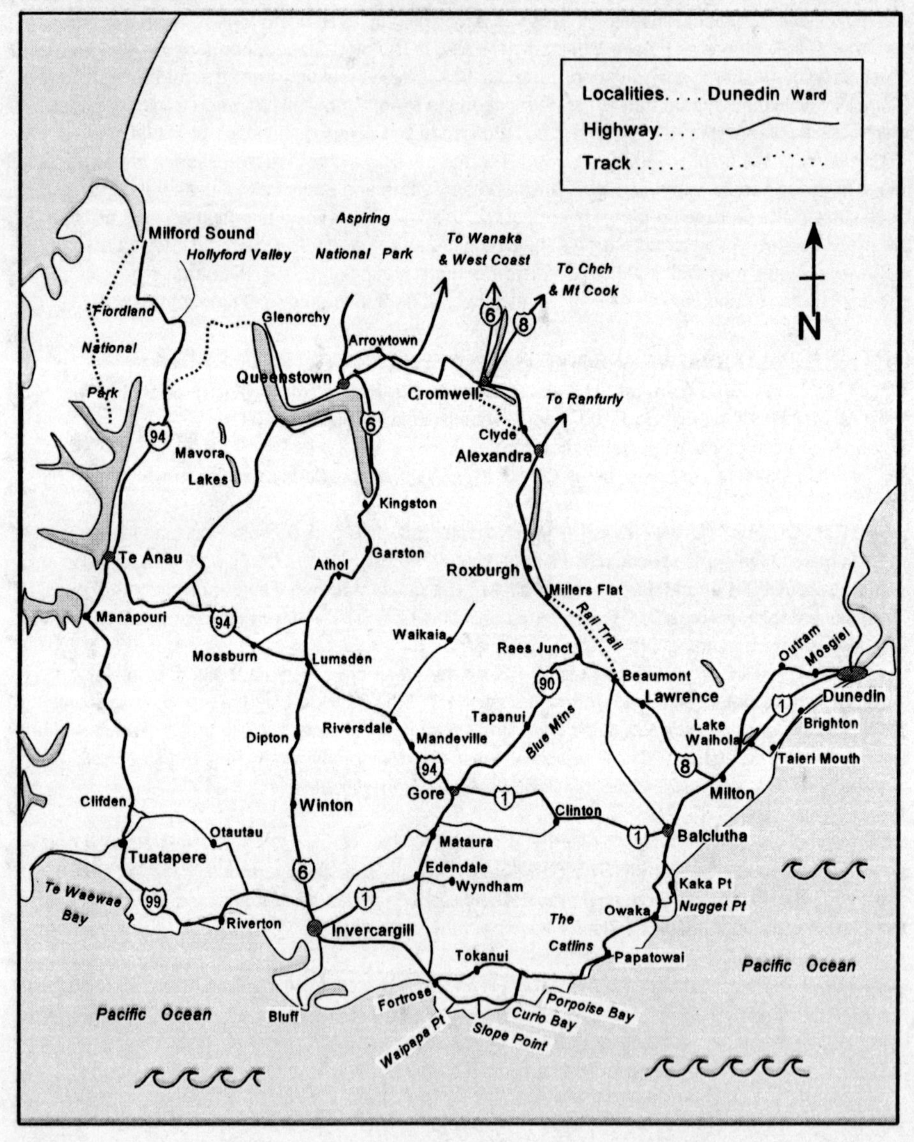

9 QUEENSTOWN - LUMSDEN - INVERCARGILL.

ROUTE: QUEENSTOWN - INVERCARGILL on SH 6. 187 km on SH 6.
LINK ROAD i LUMSDEN (SH 6) - TE ANAU on SH 94.
ii LUMSDEN (SH 6) - GORE (SH 1) on SH 94.
SIDE TRIP INVERCARGILL - STEWART ISLAND.

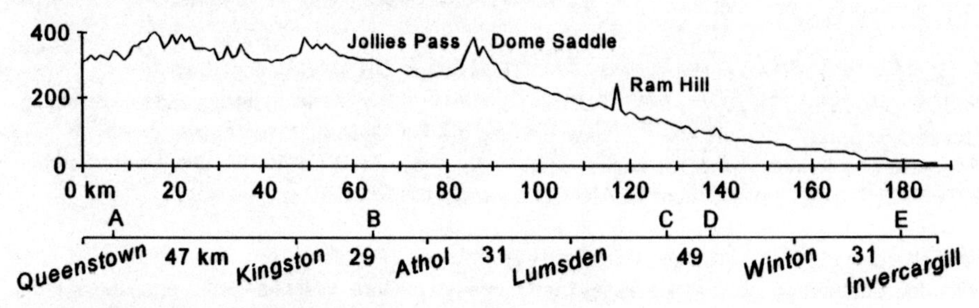

SERVICES: **QUEENSTOWN:** See pages 38-39 or 50-51.
A) FRANKTON: Alt 314m, pop 1,000. Food: All outlets. Accom: Motor camp 2, hotel.
KINGSTON: Alt 310m, pop 100. Store/tearooms, pub, motor camp. **B) GARSTON:** Alt 305m, hotel.
ATHOL: Alt 290m. Store, motor camp (no kitchen). **JOLLIES PASS:** Alt 396m, picnic area.
LUMSDEN: Alt: 200m, pop 600. ***i:*** Railway Station ☎248-7334.
Food: All outlets except supermarket. Accom: Motor camp; motel; 2 hotel.
Transport: Bus & shuttles to/from Invercargill, Qutn, Dunedin, Te Anau.
C) DIPTON: Alt 100m, dairy. **D) BENMORE:** pub.
WINTON: Alt 50m, pop 2,500. All types food of outlets. Motel. Bicycle shop.
E) LORNEVILLE: Lodge (also tent sites).
INVERCARGILL: Alt 20m, pop 57,000. ***i:*** Museum, Queens Park ☎214-6243.
Food: All outlets. Accom: 5 motor camp; hostel (3 bkpr, 1 YHA); 27 motel; 3 hotel.
Transport: Bus & shuttles to/from Dunedin, Chch, Te Anau & Qutn. Bicycle shops.

GRADIENTS: Undulates alongside Lake Wakatipu to Frankton then right (south) onto SH 6. The highway leaves the lake for 10 km to pass Kelvin Heights with a dip to cross the Kawarau River. Rejoin the lake for the rest of the 30 km to Kingston, a gentle rolling road with some steeper, longer bits around the Devil's Staircase.

After Kingston there is a short hill to climb, the terrain then becomes easier through to Lumsden with few hills apart from Dome Saddle & Jollies Pass (396m) between Athol and Five Rivers. Ram Hill is the only hill between Lumsden and Invercargill, having a quite steep 1 km climb to 240m followed by a 1½ km stepped descent. Never far from the Oreti River the gradients flatten out with traffic flows becoming heavier as Invercargill nears. SH 6 goes straight to the centre of Invercargill.

ATTRACTIONS: The highlight of the journey is at the beginning, travelling alongside Lake Wakatipu and skirting below the Remarkables with spectacular views for many kilometres until Kingston where train buffs may see and/or travel a short distance on the Kingston Flyer, a vintage steam engine, whose future seems always in doubt. Lumsden is a small pleasant rural settlement.

Apart from some gorgeous sheep in the paddocks, things become less interesting as pastoral country takes over from the high mountain ranges. SH 6 follows Oreti River from Lumsden to Invercargill, a popular fishing river. As the name suggests, Invercargill has strong Scottish links. This is a sprawling rural service city, administration centre and biggest population of Southland. In the museum see live Tuataras, modern day cousins of the dinosaurs. The even spread of rainfall throughout the year means the countryside rarely browns off as in other parts of NZ. In pre-Europeans times much of the plains around Invercargill were covered by a dense impenetrable forest of which little remains.

OPTIONS: **LINK ROAD i** LUMSDEN (SH 6) - TE ANAU on SH 94. Distance 78 km.
LUMSDEN - MOSSBURN 20 km, MOSSBURN - TE ANAU 58 km. SH 94 undulates and rolls, climbing for the middle part of the route and ending with a long gradual descent to Te Anau.
LUMSDEN: See Above. MOSSBURN: Store, tearooms, motor camp (3½ km N), bkpr hostel, hotel.
WHITESTONE RIVER: picnic area. TE ANAU: See page 43.

LINK ROAD ii LUMSDEN (SH 6) - GORE (SH 1). Distance 62 km on SH 94.
Gentle descent through the Waimea Valley from Lumsden to Gore. Waimea Plains, once forest then tussock grassland, now fertile farming country. The Hokonui Hills border to the south with remnants of native bush that once covered much of the region. 17 km from Lumsden is . . .
BALFOUR: Alt 170m. Dairy, pub. Another 15 km to . . .
RIVERSDALE: Alt 130m. Store, takeaways, tearooms, restaurant, hotel. Then 13 km to . . .
MANDEVILLE: Alt 100m, pop 150. The Croydon Aircraft Co restores vintage aircraft.
Finally 17 km more to . . . GORE: See page 46.

SIDE TRIP INVERCARGILL - STEWART ISLAND. Access by air or ferry. Another of those get away from it all places with just one small settlement at Half Moon Bay. Plenty of tramping, sea fishing and kayaking opportunities but limited cycling - there aren't many roads! Kiwis (birds) are common here. Stewart Island has NZ's latest national park.

10 QUEENSTOWN - TE ANAU - INVERCARGILL.

ROUTE:	Back Road/SH 99	SH 94
10a) WALTER PEAK - TE ANAU	114 km	
10b)TE ANAU - INVERCARGILL	186 km	
Side Trip TE ANAU - MILFORD SOUND		119 km
Total	300 km	

ALTERNATIVE 10b) CLIFDEN - OTAUTAU - RIVERTON.
SIDE TRIP 10a) TE ANAU - MILFORD SOUND on SH 94.
10b) i LAKE MANAPOURI - DEEP COVE - DOUBTFUL SOUND ii To LAKE MONOWAI.
iii CLIFDEN - LAKE HAUROKO. iv TUATAPERE - PORT CRAIG. v INVERCARGILL - BLUFF.
Note: Except to Bluff these side trips are mostly gravel roads or tracks.
LINK ROAD 10a) TE ANAU - LUMSDEN (SH 6) on SH 94. See Options above.

10a QUEENSTOWN - MAVORA LAKES - TE ANAU. 114km

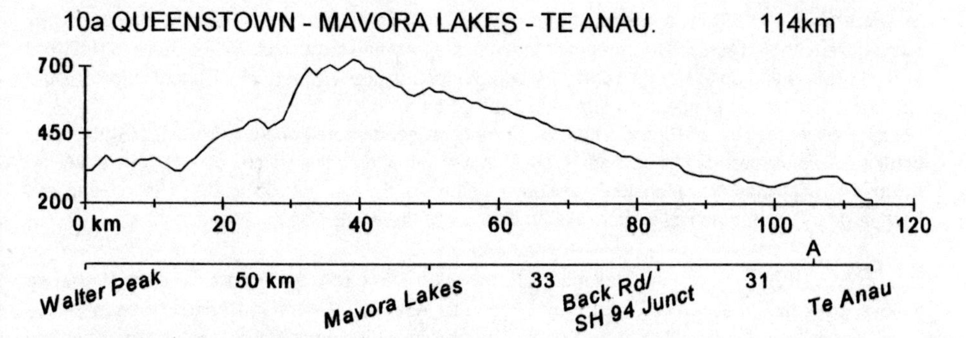

SERVICES: **MAVORA LAKES:** DoC camping (toilets, water, tables).
A) WHITESTONE RIVER: picnic area.
TE ANAU: Alt 200m, pop 1,700. ***i:*** 1) Real Journeys, Te Anau Terrace ☎249-8900 for tours.
2) DoC, Lake Front Drive ☎249-7921 for track information. Food: All outlets.
Accom: 3 motor camp; hostel (5 bkpr, 1 YHA); 10 motel; 5 hotel. Bicycle Shop.
Transport: Bus & shuttles to/from Milford Sound, Dunedin, Chch, Invercargill & Queenstown.

GRADIENTS: The Back Rd avoids much of the traffic and tourist buses that use SH 6/94. Considering it is gravel, the condition is usually quite good apart from the first part. After rolling alongside Lake Wakatipu to Mt Nicolas Station, climb sometimes steeply away from the lake along the Von River. Only one saddle to cross, then mostly flat to undulating to SH 94. A long gradual descent to Te Anau with a final small hill into the village.

ATTRACTIONS: Take the vintage steamer SS Earnslaw from Queenstown to Walter Peak Station. On a short side trip are idyllic Mavora Lakes with the Livingstone Mountains a back drop. Quiet.

10a SIDE TRIP: TE ANAU - MILFORD SOUND. 119km

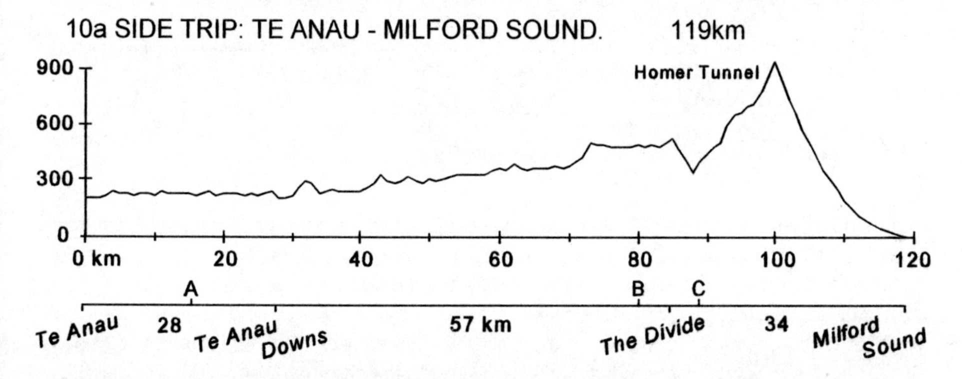

SERVICES: **TE ANAU DOWNS:** Hotel, bkpr hostel. Between 16 & 80 km from Te Anau, starting at **A) TEN MILE BUSH** & ending at **B) LAKE GUNN** are 12 DoC camp sites most with toilets,& tables.
THE DIVIDE: Alt 520m, bus shelter, water, toilets.
C) HOLLYFORD VALLEY: Gunn's Camp (also cabins, shop and museum) 8 km from SH 94.
MILFORD SOUND: Alt 10m. Restaurant, bkpr hostel (also shop & tent sites); hotel (expensive).
Note the lack of services along this route.

GRADIENTS: SH 94 is now sealed all the way to Milford Sound. Starts easy but soon becomes hilly some quite long and steep. The steepest gradients are between the Divide (520m) down to Hollyford turn off (350m) and up to Homer Tunnel (945m). A steep descent from Homer Tunnel to Milford, the last few km becoming gentle. Now turn round and go back!

Note: Beware the Homer Tunnel, a narrow 1.2 km of unlit and unlined one-way blackness with a 1:10 gradient downhill towards Milford Sound. Those not wanting to do this section can: 1) Take a day trip by bus from Te Anau or Queenstown. 2) Leave the bike at the last DoC camp site at Lake Gunn and hitch or go by bus for the last stretch. 3) Combine a visit there with tramping some tracks.

ATTRACTIONS: Fiordland National Park has high snow capped mountains, deep U shaped valleys, river flats, native bush, abundant bird life to feast the eyes on. Te Anau claims to be the "Walking capital of the World" with many tracks nearby, including three of the Great Walks. Note that huts on the Routeburn and Milford Tracks are now for the walking wallets of the world. If these appear expensive and restrictive then try others such as Greenstone/Caples or Kepler Tracks.

Some of the many scenic attractions along the highway are Mirror Lakes, Eglinton Valley, Avenue of the Disappearing Mountain, Cascade Creek, Lake Gunn, The Divide, Hollyford Valley, Homer Tunnel, The Chasm, Milford Sound with Stirling Falls & Mitre Peak. Sea kayaking is possible at Milford Sound and nearby lakes. All the lush vegetation means high rainfall.

OPTIONS: **SIDE TRIP** HOLLYFORD VALLEY to GUNN'S CAMP and the Hollyford Track along the Hollyford Valley. This tramping track goes all the way to the coast at Martin's Bay via Lake McKerrow and Jamestown. Experienced trampers can to continue on to Haast from Martin's Bay.

10b TE ANAU - TUATAPERE - INVERCARGILL. 186km

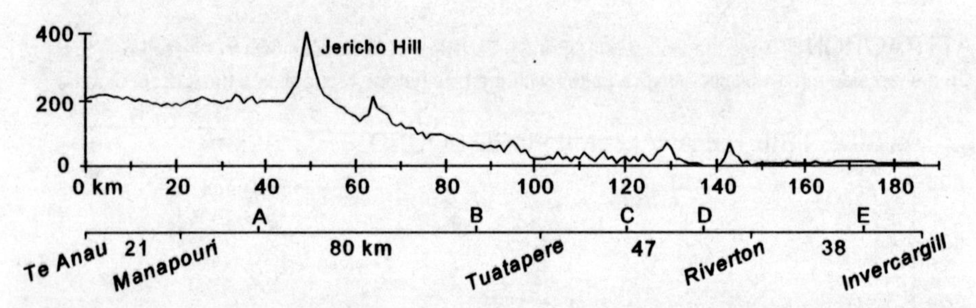

SERVICES: **TE ANAU:** See Section 10a. No services for 80 km between Manapouri & Tuatapere.
MANAPOURI: Alt 185, pop 300. Store, tearooms/dairy, restaurant, 2 motor camp, 2 bkpr hostel, hotel.
A) WHARE CREEK: picnic area. **B) CLIFDEN BRIDGE:** DoC style camping (toilets, table).
TUATAPERE: Alt 70m, pop 850. Store, takeaways, tearooms. 2 motor camp; bkpr farm, motel; hotel.
C) OREPUKI: Pub, domain camping (toilet) at nearby Monkey Island, bkpr farm hostel has closed).
D) COLAC BAY: Tearooms/dairy, hotel (also tent sites & bkpr accom).
RIVERTON: Alt 10m, pop 1800. Food: All outlets.
Accom: Motor camp; bkpr hostel; motel; hotel 3. **E) WALLACETOWN:** Dairy, takeaways, pub.
INVERCARGILL: See page 41 or 46.

GRADIENTS: Easy gradients to begin with as the highway crosses the broad plain of the Waiau Valley followed, by a couple of short steep ups and down to cross Whare Creek and climb onto the river terrace. Then gentle terrain until the 2½ km climb to cross Jericho Hill with the last 1½ km becoming steeper. The 3 km downhill begins steeply, easing to gentle undulations. Easy terrain continues, apart from a few low rolling hills near McIvors, north of Wairaki River, for the rest of the way to Tuatapere.

On leaving Tuatapere the highway continues its easy way for 10 km. It then becomes rolling as the coast nears with many ups and down most of the way to Colac Bay. Fairly flat from there for 14 km followed by a straight 1½ km climb and a 4 km descent in a series of steps to Riverton. The rest of the way to Invercargill is mostly flat as the highway crosses the broad coastal plains.
Note: The south coast is a popular area for strong westerly winds.

ATTRACTIONS: The road from Te Anau to Invercargill and Catlins is known as the Southern Scenic Route. After Te Anau comes Lake Manapouri, the second deepest and said to be the prettiest lake in NZ. Departing from the wharf are guided tours to the Manapouri Power Station and Doubtful Sound. Kayaking is possible on these lakes and sounds. Side trips off the highway go to Lakes Monowai & Hauroko, the latter being the deepest in NZ. Clifden has the historic wooden suspension bridge and limestone caves nearby.

Tuatapere is a small rural village claiming to be the sausage capital of NZ? A side trip to the Hump Ridge tramping track goes to Port Craig & Waitutu Forest at the south end of Fiordland National Park using old wooden viaducts. The Percy Burn is said to be the highest in the Southern Hemisphere. Dolphins can sometimes been seen in picturesque Te Wae Wae Bay and the distinct Monkey Island near Orepuke is of historical importance to Maori. Near windswept Colac Bay is a gold mining museum at Midlands Farm. Riverton has a pleasing ambience and claims to be the oldest European settlement in NZ, being established by whalers before 1820, originally named Jacobs River.

OPTIONS: **SIDE TRIP i** LAKE MANAPOURI - DEEP COVE & Westground Underarm Power Station by boat, then by road to DOUBTFUL SOUND over the Wilmot Pass (670m). Annual rainfall is up to 8 metres here. Access the remote Dusky Sound Track from here.

SIDE TRIP ii LAKE MONOWAI: DoC camping (toilets, water, table) by the lakeside. Lodge (also bkpr accom). Mostly gravel road, 14 km west of the highway.

SIDE TRIP iii CLIFDEN - LAKE HAUROKO: DoC camping (toilets, water, table) 6 km before the lake. 32 km west along a gravel road, this is NZ's deepest lake.

SIDE TRIP iv TUATAPERE - PORT CRAIG: DoC hut, is on the Southern Coastal or Hump Ridge Track. BLUECLIFFS BEACH: bkpr hostel. Goes along beaches and through native bush of the Waitutu Forest where the Southern Hemisphere's highest wooden viaduct at Percy Burn forms part of the route. The Hump Ridge Track has been developed to take in other natural features and avoids having to return the same way.

SIDE TRIP v INVERCARGILL - BLUFF: Alt 10m, pop 2,500. ***i:*** Marine Pde ☎212-8305.
Food: All outlets except supermarket. Accom: Motor camp; bkpr hostel; 4 hotel.

On an easy but busy road, Fred & Myrtle's Paua House is a collection of paua and other shells from around the world, hand collected by Fred himself. World famous Bluff oysters are a delicacy in season, they have a seafood festival, usually in May. Stewart Island ferry leaves from here. Bluff Pt is not the most southerly point of the Mainland, Slope Pt has that honour.

ALTERNATIVE CLIFDEN - WAIMATUKU is a quiet rolling inland route through OTAUTAU: pop 900. Store, tearooms, takeaways, restaurant, motor camp (no cabins), bkpr hostel, hotel.

11 INVERCARGILL - BALCLUTHA - DUNEDIN.

ROUITE:	SH 1	SH 92
11 INVERCARGILL - GORE - BALCLUTHA - DUNEDIN	220 km*	
11alt INVERCARGILL - OWAKA - BALCLUTHA		161 km**

* Add 9 km if going via Hedgehope (SH 96).

** 24 km longer than SH 1 & add another 15 km if going via Curio Bay.

ALTERNATIVE 11) i INVERCARGILL - GORE. SH 1 or the quiet SH 96 via Hedgehope.
ii INVERCARGILL - BALCLUTHA. The easier SH 1 through Gore or the quiet, partly gravel, hilly but more interesting SH 92 through Curio Bay and the Catlins.
iii LAKE WAIHOLA - DUNEDIN on SH 1 or quieter, partly gravel road via Taieri Mouth & Brighton.

LINK ROAD 11) i GORE (SH 1) - LUMSDEN (SH 6) on SH 94. See Options page 42.
ii GORE (SH 1) - RAES JUNCTION (SH 8) on SH 90. See Options page 50.

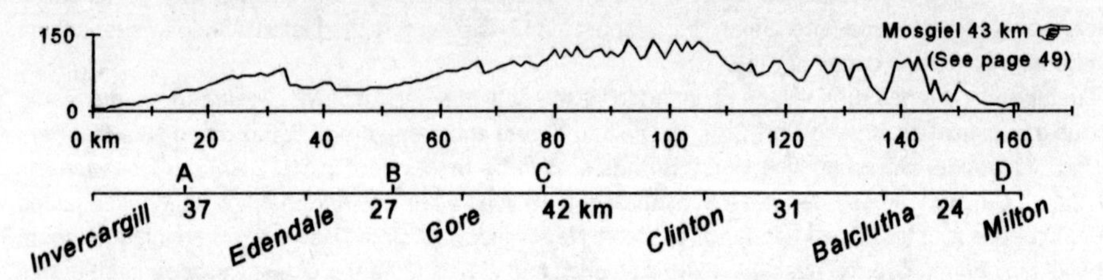

SERVICES: **INVERCARGILL:** Alt 20m, pop 57,000. ***i:*** Museum, Queens Park ☎214-6243.
Food: All outlets. Accom: 5 motor camp; hostel (3 bkpr, 1 YHA); 27 motel; 3 hotel.
Transport: Bus & shuttles to/from Dunedin, Christchurch, Te Anau & Queentown. Bicycle Shops.
A) LONGBUSH: Store, pub. **WOODLANDS:** Store, pub. **EDENDALE:** Store, cheese factory.
3 km off SH 1 to the East is **WYNDHAM:** Alt 25m, pop 750. Food: All outlets except supermarket.
Accom: Domain camping (no cabins); hotel.
B) MATAURA: Alt 50, pop 2,000. All types of food outlets except supermarket. Hotel/motel.
GORE: Alt 80m, pop 8,500. ***i:*** Cnr Medway & Ordsal Sts ☎208-9908. Food: All outlets.
Accom: Motor camp; bkpr hostel; 2 motel; hotel. Bicycle Shops.
C) PUKERAU: Tearooms. **CLINTON:** Alt: 130.Store, takeaways, bkpr hostel, hotel/motel.
BALCLUTHA: Alt 20, pop 4,000. ***i:*** 63 Clyde St ☎418-0388. Food: All outlets.
Accom: Motor camp; bkpr hostel; 3 motel; 2 hotel.
Transport: Bus & shuttles to/from Dunedin, Te Anau, Catlins & Invercargill. Bicycle Shop.
LOVELL'S FLAT: Tearooms. **D) CLARKESVILLE JUNCTION:** picnic area.
MILTON: Pop 2,000. Food: All outlets. Accom: Motor camp; bkpr hostel; motel. Bicycle shop.
LAKE WAIHOLA: Store, takeaways, pub, motor camp, motel. **EAST TAIERI:** Dairy.
MOSGIEL: Alt 10m, pop 9,200. Food: All outlets. Accom: Motel; hotel. Bicycle shop.
DUNEDIN: See pages 18-20.

GRADIENTS: SH 1 begins flat as it leaves Invercargill heading east, the only hills of note are a short ½ km descent before and after Edendale. Mostly gentle gradients all the way to Gore. After Gore the highway alternates between undulations and rolling, with some quite steep sections. A final long and quite steep descent past Peggydale arrives at Balclutha.

Depart Balclutha with a quite steep 2 km climb, then rolling with some longish and steepish hills for much of the way to Lovell's Flat. SH 1 then becomes gentle as it approaches Clarkesville. Easy gradients continue from there through Milton until Mosgiel on the outskirts of Dunedin. The hills start again at the Mosgiel turnoff. Hilly whichever way is taken into Dunedin, see pages 18-20.

ATTRACTIONS: There's not much of interest going this way. A short distance off SH 1 from Edendale is the pleasant olde worlde Wyndham whose streets are named after battles fought during the Crimea War. Gore is NZ's country music capital and Mataura River is famous for its brown trout. The giant fish in the centre of town is only a statue, so don't be afraid.

At Pukerau there is a reserve of rare red tussock adjcent to the highway. Clinton and Gore was of interest to Americans. After Balclutha is Lovells Flat, with historic Garvan House and old sod cottage. Lake Waihola and renowned Sinclair Wetlands are the main attractions of the fertile Taieri Plains.

OPTIONS: **ALTERNATIVE i** to SH 1 from INVERCARGILL - GORE is SH 96. Mostly undulates and rolls with an occasional steeper section. Much quieter than SH 1. Access is by going north a few km on SH 6 toward Queenstown then east at LORNEVILLE: Lodge (also cabins & tent sites).

ALTERNATIVE iii LAKE WAIHOLA - TAIERI MOUTH - DUNEDIN goes over a big sometimes steep hill with 10 km of the 12 km being gravel (muddy when wet) to TAIERI MOUTH (motor camp/motel). Another 35 km (all tar-sealed) goes to Dunedin along the coastline via BRIGHTON (store, motor camp). Much quieter than SH 1. After Green Island head up Kaikorai Valley Road and right onto Stuart St. Another rolling gravel road goes from Lake Waihola past SINCLAIR WETLANDS (hostel) to Mosgiel.

ALTERNATIVE ii: INVERCARGILL - CATLINS - BALCLUTHA. 161km

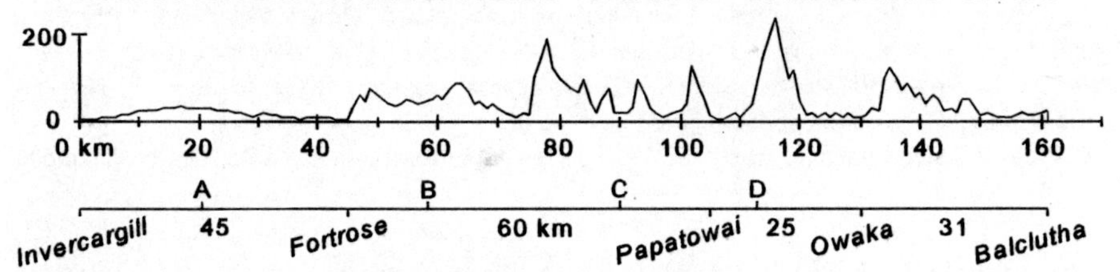

SERVICES: **INVERCARGILL:** See previous section for details. **A) MOKOTUA:** Dairy/tearooms.
FORTROSE: Alt 10m, pop 100. Picnic area & informal camping (toilet, table).
B) TOKANUI: Alt 45m, pop 150. Store, pub. **C) CHASLANDS:** Lodge. **LAKE WILKIE:** picnic area.
PAPATOWAI: Alt 20m. Motor camp/shop (no cabins); bkpr farm hostel (3 km from village); 2 motel.
PURAKAUNUI BAY: DoC camping (toilets, water) several km off SH 92.
TAWANUI: DoC camping (toilets, water) 11 km off SH 92. **D) MATAI FALLS:** picnic area.
OWAKA: Alt 20m, pop 350. *i:* Main Road ☎415-8371. Food: Store, dairy/tearooms, takeaways, pub.
Accom: 2 bkpr hostel (one 5 km away); 2 motel; hotel (also tent sites).
Transport: Shuttle to/from Dunedin & Invercargill (not every day).
POUNAWEA: DoC Motor Camp (4 km off SH 92 from Owaka).
BALCLUTHA: See previous section for details.

GRADIENTS: Head south towards Bluff on SH 1 for 2 km and go left (east) onto SH 92. Begins flat as it leaves Invercargill with few undulations to speak of most of the way to Fortrose. Although no high passes to cross the road has plenty of rolling hills to negotiate, with some quite steep ups and down occasionally climbing to 200m such as Chaslands, Florence Hill & Table Hill.

The 21 km of gravel remaining between Waikawa Harbour turn-off and Papatowai is scheduled to be completely tar-sealed by the end of 2004. After Owaka is the moderately steep MacDonald's Hill, then the highway rolls before becoming flat as it nears Balclutha.

ATTRACTIONS: The Catlins Coast has many interesting natural and historical features. If you decide to go this way it is suggested not to rush through because many of the attractions are several kms off SH 92 down gravel side roads.

Like many other places in the south, whaling and gold mining formed the basis of early development followed by forestry and then farming, when much of the extensive native forests were cleared.

At Fortrose an ALTERNATIVE route goes to Curio Bay and rejoins SH 92 shortly after Waikawa Harbour, (see below for services on this alternative to an alternative!). There are still about 13 km of gravel on this route. A 3 km side trip goes to Waipapa Pt lighthouse where in 1881 NZ suffered its worst shipping disaster when 131 people died in the *Tararua*. Another 8 km side trip is to Slope Pt, the South Island's southern point, not Bluff as commonly believed. Beyond is Curio Bay, where one of the world's best examples of an ancient 180 million year old petrified Jurassic forest is visible at low tide. Dolphins sometimes body surf in the breakers in adjacent Porpoise Bay and it may be possible to join them. Penguins and seals also inhabit much of the coastline. Services include....

SLOPE POINT: 3 km N is a farm hostel/tent sites/small shop/info centre.

WAIPOHATU: Recreational Reserve DoC style camping (toilets, water, tables) near Haldane.

CURIO BAY: Motor camp (small shop, no cabins), bkpr hostel 2.

WAIKAWA BAY: Motor camp, bkpr hostel.

Beyond Waikawa Bay, the Catlins area has several more scenic beauties including Niagara Falls (yes it's true!), McLean Falls, Cathedral Caves (access only at low tide), Purakaunui Falls, Tahakopa Bay, Fleming River, Lake Wilkie, Florence Hill, Tautuku Beach, Papatowai, Owaka, Pounawea, Matai Falls, Tunnel Hill. There is also a not particularly interesting walkway alongside the Catlins River.

After Owaka there is yet another alternative to this alternative route (confused? So am I!) This time it goes via Kaka Point and nuggety Nugget Point, the latter being a scenic reserve.

KAKA POINT: Dairy/takeaways, several DoC camp sites (table, toilet), motor camp, bkpr hostel, motel.

12 DUNEDIN - ROXBURGH - QUEENSTOWN.

ROUTE:	SH1/8/6
12a) DUNEDIN - ROXBURGH	155 km
12b) ROXBURGH - QUEENSTOWN	134 km
Total	289 km

ALTERNATIVE 12a) MOSGIEL - ALEXANDRA. SH 1 & 8 via Roxburgh or quieter SH 87/85 through Middlemarch & Ranfurly. See pages 21-23. These routes do not meet at any point until Alexandra.

i DUNEDIN - MOSGIEL - LAKE WAIHOLA SH 1 or coastal Southern Scenic Route through Taieri Mouth.or past the renowned Sinclair Wetlands See Alternative iii above

12b) i ALEXANDRA - CLYDE SH6, River Track or Earnscleugh Rd.

ii CLYDE - CROMWELL SH6 or gravel Hawksburn Road through Bannockburn.

iii ARROWTOWN - QUEENSTOWN SH 6 or quieter Malagan Road.

SIDE TRIP 12b) i QUEENSTOWN - GLENORCHY. ii SKIPPER'S CANYON.

LINK ROAD 12a) RAES JUNCTION (SH 8) - TAPANUI - GORE (SH 1) on SH 90.

12a DUNEDIN - MILTON - ROXBURGH. 155km

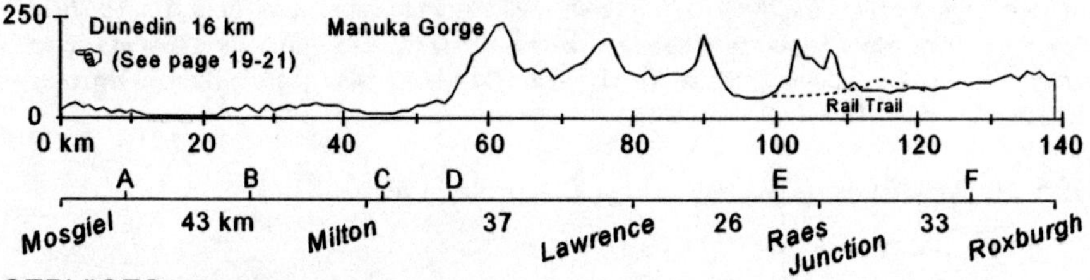

250
Dunedin 16 km
(See page 19-21)
Manuka Gorge
Rail Trail
0
0 km 20 40 60 80 100 120 140
A B C D E F
Mosgiel 43 km Milton 37 Lawrence 26 Raes Junction 33 Roxburgh

SERVICES: **DUNEDIN:** See pages 18-20.
MOSGIEL: Alt 10m, pop 9,200. Food: All outlets. Accom: Motel; hotel. Bicycle Shop.
EAST TAIERI: Dairy. **A) ALLENTON:** picnic area.
B) LAKE WAIHOLA: Store, takeaways, pub, motor camp; motel.
MILTON: Pop 2,000. Food: All outlets. Accom: Motor camp; bkpr hostel; motel. Bicycle shop.
C) CLARKESVILLE JUNCTION: picnic area. **D) MANUKA GORGE:** picnic area.
LAWRENCE: Alt 110m, pop 600. Food: All outlets except supermarket.
Accom: Motor camp; bkpr hostel; 2 motel.
E) BEAUMONT: Alt 75m. Hotel (also tent sites). **RAES JUNCTION:** Alt 130m, pub.
MILLER'S FLAT: Alt 85m. Dairy, pub, motor camp. **F) ETTRICK:** Alt 90m. Dairy/tearooms, pub.
ROXBURGH: Alt 140m, pop 700. *i*:120 Scotland St ☎446-8920. Food: All outlets except supermarket.
Accom: Motor camp; bkpr hostel; 2 motel.

GRADIENTS: See pages 18-20 for details on Dunedin. Go through Mosgiel and right onto SH 1. Mostly gentle gradients from there while crossing the Taieri Plains through Milton to Clarkesville Junction to join SH 8. The first few kms are almost flat as the highway heads inland. It then climbs variable steep for 7 km through Manuka Gorge to Round Hill, from where it drops steeply, then rolls and undulations down to Waitahuna and continues rolling on to Lawrence.

Apart from a flattish area around Lawrence the highway rolls and undulates to Beaumont, then the hills become longer and steeper and more winding until 5 km beyond Raes Junction at Island Block. On emerging from the hills gradients level out as SH 8 travels near Clutha River to Roxburgh. Only the last few km are gently rolling.

ATTRACTIONS: On the Taieri Plains is Lake Waihola and nearby world renowned Sinclair Wetlands. Pass through scenic Manuka Gorge and the way to Lawrence. Nearby Gabriels Gully was the site of the first gold rush in 1861 and named after the gentleman credited with the find. At its peak 11,000 prospectors lived there, twice the size of Dunedin at the time. They extracted 200,000 ounces of gold during the first year. Like many other towns founded during the gold rush, Lawrence became a sleepy backwater servicing local farms. Try the rail trail between Beaumont and Miller's Flat that follows the Clutha River's eastern bank, passes through a scenic gorge and the historic Lonely Graves. Continue on the same side along Teviot Road to Roxburgh and Roxbugh Hydro.

Almost the entire Central Otago region owes its development to gold discovered here in large quantities in the 1860's. There are a number of Otago Goldfields Park sites strung along or near the highway as reminders of those pioneering days. When the gold ran out, horticulture and sheep have become important parts of the Central Otago economy. Apricots and a variety of stone and pip fruits are harvested in summer and autumn with seasonal work available. Can be hot in summer.

OPTIONS: **LINK ROAD** RAES JUNCTION (SH 8) - TAPANUI - GORE (SH 1) on SH 90, 64 km. 20 km from Raes Junct to BLACK GULLY: Recreation Reserve (cabins, no kitchen). Then 9 km to TAPANUI: Alt 190m. Store, tearooms, takeaways, caravan park (no kitchen), hotel. Tapanui's claim to fame is having a strain of flu named after it and has the Blue Mountains nearby. Then 30 km to SH 1 before a final 5 km into GORE: See page 46.

12b. ROXBURGH - CROMWELL - QUEENSTOWN. 134km

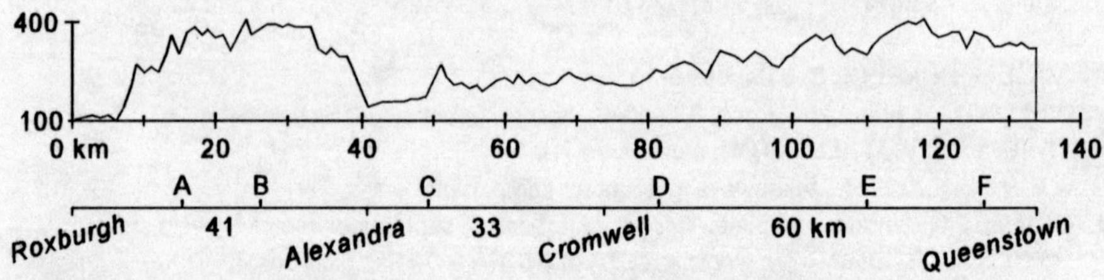

SERVICES: **ROXBURGH:** See previous section. **A) SHINGLE CREEK:** Pub, picnic area. **GORGE CREEK**: picnic area (tables, monument). **B) FRUITLANDS:** Tearooms/restaurant.

ALEXANDRA: Alt 150m, pop 5,000. ***i:*** 22 Centennial Ave ☎448-9515.
Food: All outlets. Accom: 2 motor camp; 7 motel; hotel. Bicycle Shop.

C) CLYDE: Alt 170m. All types of food outlets except supermarket. Motor camp; 2 motel; bkpr hostel.

LAKE DUNSTAN: picnic areas at Dairy Creek (also toilets), Champagne Creek & Jacksons.

CROMWELL: Alt 220m, pop 3,300. ***i:*** 47 The Mall ☎445-0212. Food: All outlets.
Accom: 4 motor camp (2 at Bannockburn); 6 motel; 2 hotel.
Transport: Bus & shuttles to/from Chch, Queenstown, Dunedin & Fox.

D) KAWARAU GORGE: Mining centre tearooms, gold panning. **CAMP CREEK:** picnic area.

E) KAWARAU BRIDGE: bungy jumping, toilets. **LAKE HAYES:** Alt 320m, motel, picnic area.

F) FRANKTON: Alt 314m, pop 1,000. Food: All outlets. Accom: 2 motor camp, hotel.

QUEENSTOWN: Alt 310m, pop 5,000. ***i:*** 1) Cnr Shotover & Camp St ☎442-4100 for tours.
2) DoC, 37 Shotover St ☎442-7933 for track information. Food: All outlets.
Accom: 4 motor camp; hostel (13 bkpr, 2 YHA); lotsa motel; many hotel. Bicycle shop.
Transport: Bus & shuttles to/from Chch, Invercargill, Milford Sound, Fox & Dunedin.

GRADIENTS: A gentle climb begins to Roxburgh Hydro then up variable steep for 3 km. Enter rolling country sometimes quite long and steep much of the way to Alexandra, ending with a long rolling descent. The gradients are gentle to Clyde whether using the rail trail or SH 8. At Clyde is a 1 km quite steep climb to join new Lake Dunstan. Going through Clyde and taking the dam road reduces the elevation gain. At the top long sweeping rolls skirt alongside the lake going all the way to Cromwell, the town centre is 1 km off SH 6 across the bridge.

Departing Cromwell the highway begins flattish before heading up-river into the narrow steep-sided Kawarau Gorge. SH 6 is now fully cleared after a huge rock slide (estimated 10,000m³) at Nevis Bluff closed the highway in October 2000 for several weeks. Hopefully you won't disappear under another one! Moderately steep and sometimes long rolls track uphill for much of the way to Kawarau Bridge. Fairly gentle rolls and undulations from there to Frankton except for a moderate climb and short downhill at Lake Hayes and dip to cross the Shotover River. After Frankton the road undulates beside Lake Wakatipu, run the gauntlet of urban traffic into Queenstown. There is cycle path between Frankton and Queenstown or try the quieter Arrowtown alternative see Options Alternative on page 54.

ATTRACTIONS: Pass Roxburgh Hydro, another man-made lake to generate electricity and more Otago Goldfields sites such as Mitchells Cottage at Fruitlands. Alexandra is the administrative centre of Central Otago has a rock around the clock, blossom festival in spring and ice skating in winter. It is fast becoming a very popular mountain biking area, with lots of old trails around the district. Among them are Graveyard Gully and Coronary Classic!

Clyde is a charming place despite the dam looming over it, the lookout has spectacular views of the area. The old Cromwell Gorge has now become the new Lake Dunstan. Filled in 1992, years late with huge cost over-runs this marvel of modern engineering seemed it would never be completed. Ponder as you pedal alongside the lake what might happen if the two fault lines the dam is built on suddenly move or the unstable hill sides slide into to lake.

Nibble on the giant fruit at the entrance to Cromwell. A town transformed from a tatty backwater into a fancy lakeside resort and fruit growing centre. Seems a little out of place somehow. Never mind, nearby Bannockburn has several historical gold rush sites and buildings.

Travel through the stark spectacular Kawarau Gorge passing more old gold mining sites, a bungy jumping bridge for those people with a deprived childhood, vineyards and pretty Lake Hayes before arriving at Queenstown. The undisputed tourist mecca of NZ, this town has a mind boggling array of activities on which to blow your budget and locals expert at helping. Access to Mt Aspiring National Park & some of the tramping tracks from Queenstown. Central Otago can be hot and dry in summer and very cold in winter (they put the beer in the fridge to stop it freezing!).

OPTIONS: **ALTERNATIVE i** ALEXANDRA - CLYDE The gravel single-track River Trail. It follows the west bank of the Clutha River all the way to Clyde. Recommended only to be used in dry weather on lightly loaded bikes. Otherwise use the nearby Earnscleugh Road.

ALTERNATIVE ii CLYDE - CROMWELL. Distance 40 km. On the gravel Hawksburn Road. For the adventurous! DoC have also developed a mountain bike trail over Cairnmuir Mountains, which runs between Hawksburn Road and Lake Dustan. For both tracks use DoC's Cairnmuir Hill Track info sheet. Begin with a challenging 150m climb in 1 km (yes) to the Clyde Lookout then easing to only a very steep 200m in 2 km. Long rolling uphills follow with a long swoop down to Bannockburn. It is better going from Cromwell to Clyde, but make sure your brakes work properly! For bikes carrying light loads!

SIDE TRIP i QUEENSTOWN - Mt ASPIRING National Park. This park borders Fiordland National Park and has more of the same spectacular scenery (less the fiords). Several tramping tracks traverse area including Routeburn and Milford. If these appear expensive and restrictive, then try others such as Greenstone/Caples or Rees/Dart Tracks. The base for exploring the many tramping tracks and last stop for supplies before heading into the mountains is . . .

GLENORCHY: ***i:*** DoC, Main Rd ☎442-9937. Takeaways, tearooms, restaurant. Motor camp (also small expensive shop), hotel. Shuttle to/from Queenstown and the tracks during the tramping season.

Travel west alongside Lake Wakatipu on a no exit road for 47 km with the lake and distant mountains always visible. The highway is now sealed all the way to Glenorchy. Undulates and steep rolls much of the way such as at 12 mile & Bennett's Bluffs. Can be busy in summer.

SIDE TRIP ii QUEENSTOWN - SKIPPER'S CANYON. Part way up Coronet Peak Road a narrow tortuous gravel road branches off to go to Skipper's Canyon. Once an important gold mining area it was one of the richest fields in the country. Very spectacular scenery but dangerous road. Four wheel drive tours, white water rafting and helicopter rides are activities available.

WEST

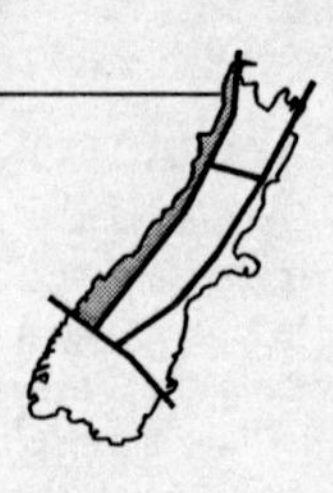

HIGHLIGHTS (not in any order of preference)

Fox, Franz & Westland National Park
Mt Aspiriing National Park
Pancake Rocks & Paparoa National Park
Welcome Flat on the Copland Track
Lakes Wanaka & Hawea
Okarito
Hokitika Greenstone
Knight's Point & Lake Paringa
Haast Pass & Makarora
Karamea & Kahurangi

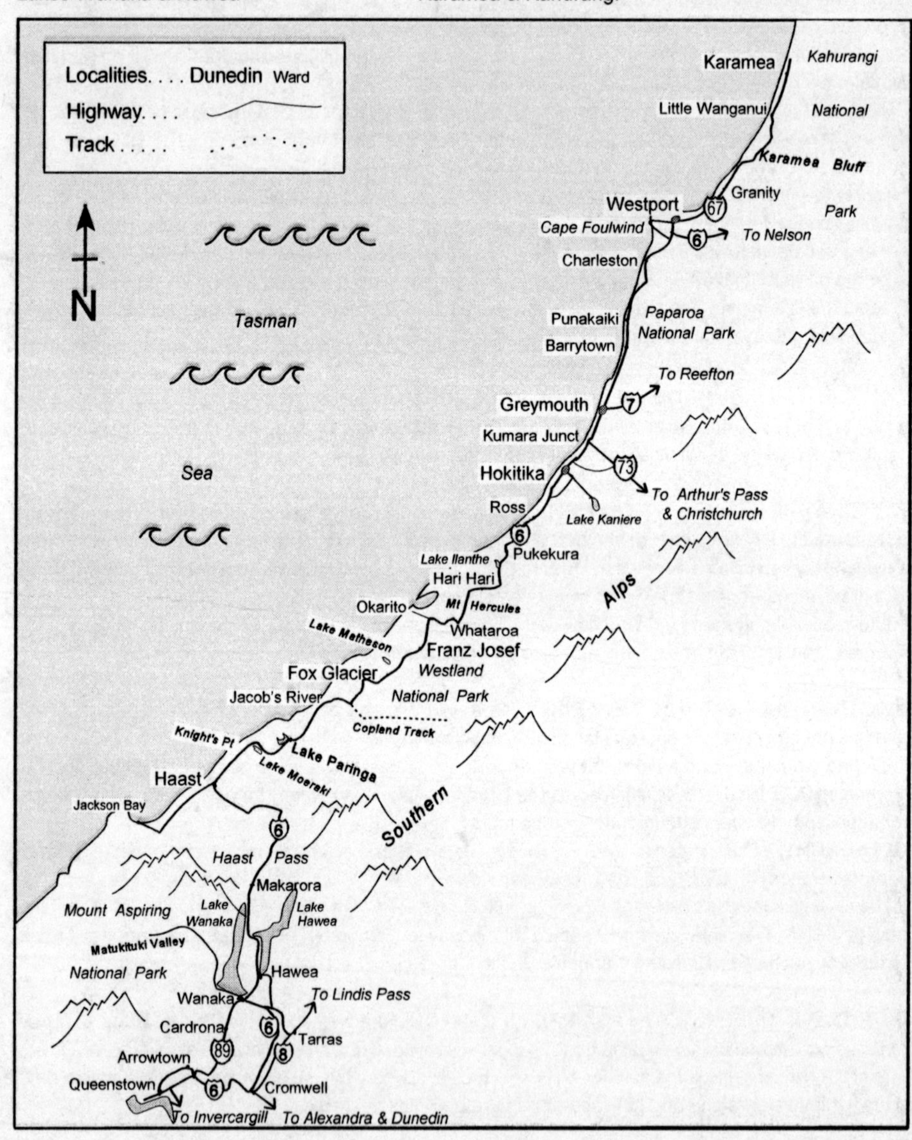

13 QUEENSTOWN - WANAKA.

ROUTE: SH 6 Malaghan Rd/SH 89

QUEENSTOWN - WANAKA 112 km* 77 km

* Add 7 km if taking Arrowtown/Malaghan Road option.

ALTERNATIVE QUEENSTOWN - WANAKA. The easier SH 6 via Cromwell or the quiet Malaghan Rd to Arrowtown and challenging, SH 89 over the Crown Range through Cardrona.
Both routes meet at the junction of SH 6 & 89 near Lake Hayes & at Wanaka.
SIDE TRIP 13) WANAKA - MT ASPIRING NAT PARK & Matukituki Valley.
13 alt) i SKIPPERS CANYON & Coronet Peak. ii ARROWTOWN - MACETOWN.
Note: These are all mostly gravel roads or tracks.

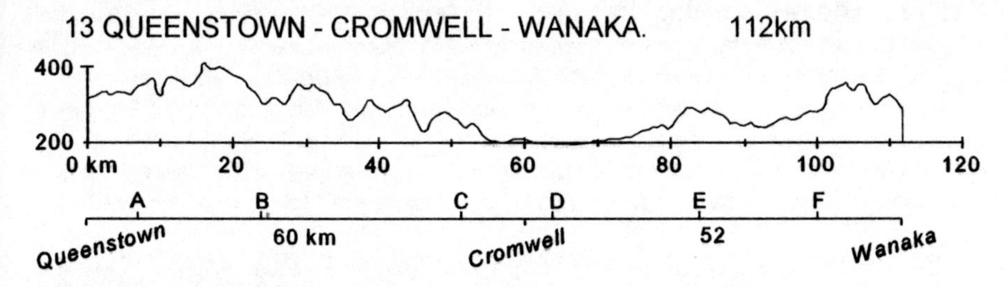

SERVICES: **QUEENSTOWN:** See page 50 (South) or page 38 (Central).
A) FRANKTON: Alt 314m, pop 1,000. Food: All outlets. Accom: Motor camp 2, hotel.
LAKE HAYES: Alt 320m, motel, picnic area. **B) KAWARAU BRIDGE:** bungy jumping, toilets.
CAMP CREEK: picnic area. **C) KAWARAU GORGE:** Mining centre tearooms.
CROMWELL: Alt 220m, pop 3,300. ***i:*** 47 The Mall ☎445-0212. Food: All outlets.
Accom: 4 motor camp (2 at Bannockburn); 6 motel; 2 hotel.
Transport: Bus & shuttles to/from Chch, Queenstown, Dunedin & Fox.
D) LOWBURN: picnic area (toilets, water, table). **E) SCHOOLHOUSE BURN:** picnic area.
F) LUGGATE: Alt 250m, pop 300. Store, pub. Domain camping. **WANAKA:** See page 56.

GRADIENTS: Run the gauntlet of the urban traffic as SH 6 undulates alongside Lake Wakatipu to Frankton, or try the cycle path. Then fairly gentle undulations apart from the dip to cross the Shotover River and a climb at Lake Hayes. This is followed by a varible downhill past SH 89 turn off then undulates for 5 km to Kawarau Bridge. The road rolls and undulates down through the Kawarau Valley from here (but with some uphill bits), part of it through the spectacular, narrow, steep-sided Kawarau Gorge. SH 8 is now fully cleared after a huge rock slide (estimated 10,000m^3) at Nevis Bluff closed the highway in October 2000 for several weeks. Hopefully you won't disappear under another one!

After emerging from the gorge the highway becomes flatter to Cromwell, the town centre being 1 km off SH 6. Easy gradients most of the way to Wanaka except for a few rolling hills between Mt Pisa & Queensberry Stations, a short steep climb after Luggate and moderate rolling hills for the last part to Wanaka. Central Otago can get hot and dry in summer.

ATTRACTIONS: Pass pretty Lake Hayes, vineyards, orchards and a bungy jumping bridge (for those people with a deprived childhood) before going through the Kawarau Valley. Jet boating, gold panning and demonstrations are at the reconstructed Kawarau Gorge Mining Centre, one of the many Otago Goldfields Park sites that dot the region. Cromwell, once a gold mining centre is now an important fruit producing region on the shores of the new Lake Dunstan with water sports & fishing the main attractions. After Cromwell there is little except sheep stations and Luggate Village until Wanaka.

Wanaka is a year round resort in a beautiful setting. It is a base for many activities like mountain biking, water sports, tramping, skiing, climbing, horse riding & scenic flights. Unusual ones being water sledging, aerobatic bi-plane rides and canyoning. There is a Warbirds Museum with occasional flying displays of their vintage aircraft and NZ's original maze and puzzle centre. This is also the gateway to Matukituki Valley & Mt Aspiring National Park, a rock climbing area of high repute.
Note: Wanaka has the last banks until Hokitika over 400 km away.

OPTIONS: **SIDE TRIP** WANAKA. - MT ASPIRING NATIONAL PARK. The gravel begins 13 km from Wanaka at GLENDHU BAY: Motor camp. Pass the turn off to Diamond Lake Walk & Treble Cone Ski Field. The not too difficult road ends after 45 km at RASPBERRY CREEK: car park (toilet).

No bikes on national park tracks so walk from there deeper into Matukituki Valley & Mt Aspiring National Park. Plenty of climbing and tramping opportunities available. Details from Wanaka DoC Visitor Centre. See the spectacular Rob Roy Glacier on a side trip up the Rob Roy Valley. Access the Rees/Dart Valleys over Cascade Saddle. Overnight stays possible at Aspiring Huts, no shops.

13 ALTERNATIVE: QUEENSTOWN - CARDRONA - WANAKA. 77km

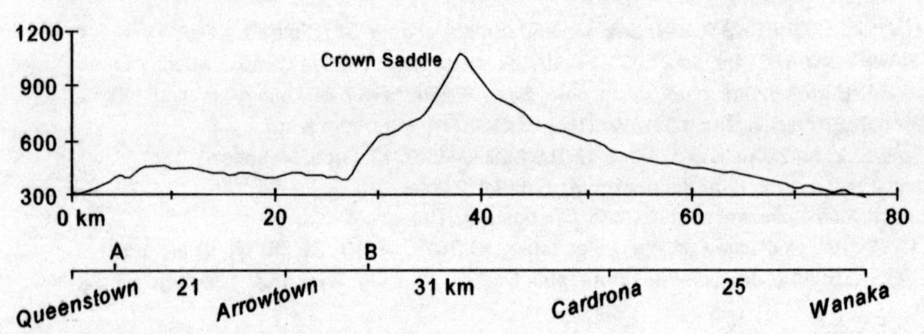

SERVICES: **QUEENSTOWN:** See pages 50-51 or pages 38-39.
A) ARTHUR'S POINT: Motor camp; hotel.
ARROWTOWN: Alt 420m, pop 1,100. ***i:*** Museum, Buckingham St ☎442-1824.
Food: All outlets except supermarket. Accom: Motor camp; 2 bkpr hostel; 4 motel; hotel.
B) PLANE TABLE: picnic area. **CARDRONA:** Alt 550m. Hotel. **WANAKA:** See page 56.

GRADIENTS: Apart from the descent and ascent to cross the Shotover River at Arthurs Point the gradients are fairly easy through to Arrowtown and continue almost flat to SH 6. Go left a short distance and left onto SH 89. Immediately begins a stiff 3 km climb through several switchbacks to a plane. It then undulates up across Crown Terrace for 5 km before starting another stiff 3½ km climb up a narrow winding road, the top being the highest highway in New Zealand at 1080m.

The descent from the Crown Range begins quite steeply, twisting down through the narrow upper Cardrona Valley for the first few kilometres. The gradients gradually ease, at Cardrona the valley broadens and terrain becomes a mostly gentle descent. On leaving Cardrona Valley the mountains fall back further and the road undulates until a final quite steep descent to enter Wanaka township. The highway is now all tar-sealed.

ATTRACTIONS: At Arthur's Pt is the Oxenbridge Tunnel, started in 1907 to divert the water to get at gold on the river bed. Taking 4 years to complete it was a financial disaster and is now used for rafting. Arrowtown is a picturesque village and very different to its near neighbour Queenstown. Worth a visit, especially in autumn when poplars become a blaze of gold. Here was once the centre of a major gold rush, Arrowtown retains the period atmosphere of the time. See the interesting museum and reconstructed Chinatown. Activities include horse treks, gold panning and several walks of varying length. After the switch-backs on SH 89 a plane table has the names of surrounding mountains. Stunning views get better all the way up to the top. Ski in winter on the mountains around Cardrona, including the only commercial nordic ski area in NZ. The historic hotel was built in 1865 at the height of yet another gold rush. After Cardrona keep an eye out for the bra fence. Wanaka is a popular year round resort in a beautiful setting. See Section 13 above for Wanaka details, Section 14a for Services.

OPTIONS: **SIDE TRIP i** QUEENSTOWN - SKIPPER'S CANYON. See page 51.

SIDE TRIP ii ARROWTOWN - MACETOWN another ghost town from the gold rush era of last century. Walk or cycle up the old rough track for about 14 km, crossing more than 40 fords of the Arrow River. Ask locally for directions and up to date conditions. No services.

14 WANAKA - HAAST - FRANZ JOSEF.

ROUTE:	SH 6
14a) WANAKA - HAAST	145 km
14b) HAAST - FRANZ JOSEF	<u>142 km</u>
Total	287 km

SIDE TRIP 14b) i HAAST - JACKSON BAY. ii FOX - GILLESPIES BEACH.

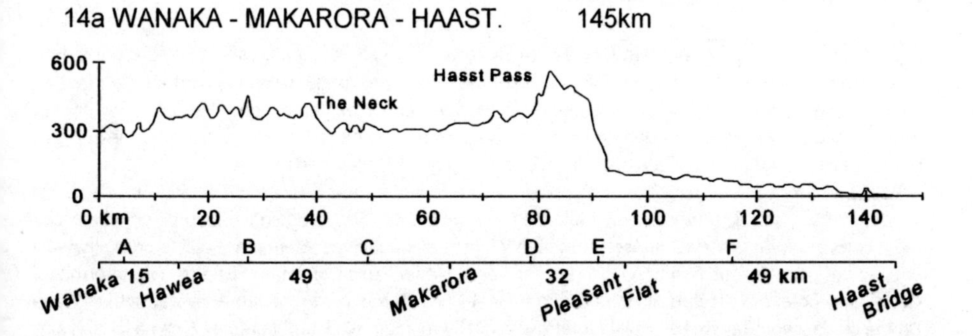

SERVICES: **WANAKA:** Alt 275m, pop 1,500. ***i:*** DoC, Ardmore St ☎443-1233 for tramping or the Lake Front for tours. Food: All outlets. Note: Wanaka has the last banks until Hokitika.
Accom: 3 motor camp; hostel (5 bkpr, 1 YHA); 12 motel; 4 hotel.
Transport: Bus & shuttle to/from Fox, Queenstown, Chch, & Dunedin. Bicycle shop.
A) ALBERT TOWN: DoC camping (toilet, water). Bkpr hostel.
LAKE HAWEA: Alt 350m, pop 300. Store/tearooms, motor camp, motel, hotel.
B) HAWEA LOOKOUT: Alt 470m, picnic area. **KIDD'S BUSH:** DoC camping, (water, toilet, shelter) 6 km off SH 6 on gravel track. **C) BOUNDARY CREEK:** DoC camping (water, toilets, shelter, sandflies).
MAKARORA: Alt 310m, pop 60. ***i:*** DoC, Main Road ☎443-8365. Store/tearooms/motel/motor camp. Beware: backpacker buses may stay overnight here. **BOILER FLAT:** picnic area.
CAMERON FLAT: Alt 335m, DoC camping. (water, toilet, sandflies).
D) DAVIS FLAT: Alt 380m, picnic area. **HAAST PASS:** Alt 563m, picnic area.
E) GATES OF HAAST: picnic area.
PLEASANT FLAT: Alt 100m, DoC camping (water, toilets, table, shelter, sandflies).
F) ROARING BILLY: picnic area.
HAAST: Alt 10m, pop 250. ***i:*** DoC, Haast Bridge ☎750-0809. Food: Takeaways, restaurant, store, pub. Accom: 2 motor camp (one at Okuru 15 km south on Jackson Bay Rd); bkpr & YHA hostel; 3 motel; hotel. Transport: Bus & shuttle to/from Fox and Queenstown.

GRADIENTS: Strong north westerly winds can be a problem between Wanaka and Haast. Predominantly moderate rolling terrain with some substantial climbs and descents such as between Albert Town and Hawea, at Hawea Lookout (470m) and The Neck (405m). After The Neck SH 6 returns to Lake Wanaka with a 5 km gradual downhill to Camp Creek, then rolling to Wharf Creek, near the head of the lake. This is followed by mostly flat to Makarora.

Beyond Makarora SH 6 alternates between uphill through beech forest and gentle undulations over open river flats, the valley becomes narrower and mountains close in up to Davis Flat. At Davis Flat the road climbs through the forest, steadily and quite steeply, except to cross two streams, for 3½ km with the last 1 km the steepest, to Haast Pass (563m). This is the lowest mountain pass to/from the West Coast over the Southern Alps.

Quite steep down for 1 km then gently for 5½ km. Becomes a steep descent for 4 km as it goes through the Gates of Haast to Thunder Creek Falls (120m). The road then flattens out, undulating gently down for the next 52 km travelling alongside Haast River to the coast with only an occasional short hill to climb on the way. The last stretches of highway between the Neck and Haast Pass have been sealed. No services for the 81 km between Makarora & Haast.

ATTRACTIONS: Albert Town Recreation Reserve is a historical gold rush site where once dwelt a large population. Between Lake Hawea and Haast there are many natural splendours to feast the eyes on, swift flowing rivers, snow capped mountains, alpine meadows, beautiful lakes and beech forest. Makarora has jet boat rides and scenic flights and is the base for exploring the northern region of Mount Aspiring National Park such as Wilkin and Young Valley systems.

After Makarora pass many scenic reserves, some include short walks such as Blue Pools, Bridal Track, Fantail and Thunder Creek Falls and Roaring Billy. The brooding, steep-sided, bush-clad mountains are ever present. Haast offers plenty of aquatic activities. Things are a little complicated & spread out here; Haast Township is 2½ km towards Haast Pass from Haast Bridge. The information centre and hotel are located at Haast Bridge. Haast Beach has a general store, 4 km south of Haast Bridge on Jackson Bay Road, Haast motor camp is 15 km south at Okuru! In recent times a local farmer came to national prominence for cutting down some ancient rain forest trees on his land - for firewood!

14b HAAST - FOX GLACIER - FRANZ JOSEF. 142km

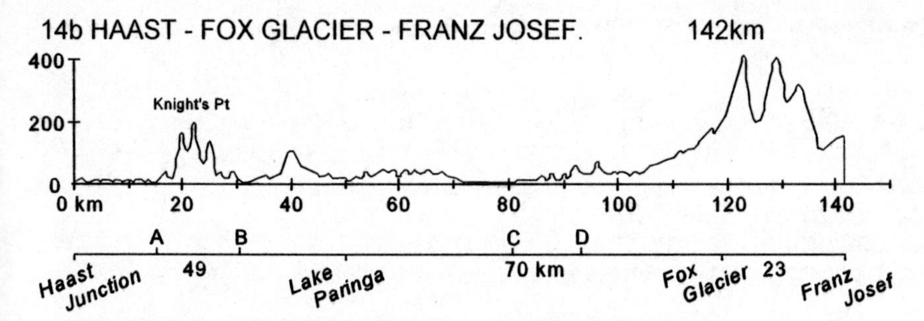

SERVICES: **HAAST:** See previous section. **WAITA RIVER:** picnic area.
A) SHIP CREEK: picnic area (shelter, toilets & tables, sandflies). **KNIGHT'S POINT:** picnic area (tables, toilets, monument). **B) LAKE MOERAKI:** Lodge (guest restaurant, motel & cottages).
LAKE PARINGA: Alt 100m, DoC camping (toilets, water, tables), 2 km N is a lodge (tearooms, restaurant, motel) might be seasonal. **BRUCE BAY:** Takeaways?, picnic area.
C) JACOB'S RIVER: Motel/cabins/tentsites (3 km N). **D) KARANGARUA RIVER:** Copland bus shelter.
FOX GLACIER: Alt 175m, pop 300. ***i:*** DoC, Main Rd ☎751-0807. Food: All outlets except supermarket. Accom: 2 motor camp; 2 bkpr hostel; 6 motel; 2 hotel.
FRANZ JOSEF GLACIER: Alt 150m, pop 350. ***i:*** DoC, Main Rd ☎752-0796.
Food: All outlets except supermarket. Accom: Motor camp; hostel (3 bkpr, 1 YHA); 9 motel; 2 hotel.
Transport: Bus & shuttle to/from Fox and Queenstown.
*Warning: Backpacker buses overnight at Franz Josef.

GRADIENTS: Quite easy gradients from Haast Bridge for the 32 km to Lake Moeraki, except for three steep hills (in 8 kms) of Knights Point between Bishops Folly and Murphy Creek. The road is narrow winding and climbs to 200m. Lake Moeraki has an easy 3 km lakeside ride, then undulates and rolls 18 km to Lake Paringa with another similar 6 km to Paringa River. The 63 km from there to Fox are generally flat to undulating, apart from short rolling hills each side of Karangarua River.

Between Fox to Franz there are three major hills of the Cook (410m) Waikukupa (405m) and Omoeroa (320m) Saddles to cross for the first 18 km of the 23 km. Apart from the last climb, each hill has an elevation gain/loss of 200m. The road is often steep, narrow and winding.

ATTRACTIONS: Travel up the narrow West Coast corridor, sea to the west, the mountains always a backdrop to the east. Go through dense rain forests, passing river flats, dark still lakes, isolated farms and tiny settlements. Occasionally touch the coast with the seascapes of Ship Creek, Knights Point & Bruce Bay. As with many hilly sections in the South Island, the views make the effort rewarding and Knight's Pt is no exception. Pass the forest fringed lakes of Moeraki & Paringa. Karangarua River is the start of the Copland Track to the hot springs at Welcome Flat. The Copland Pass beyond is an alpine pass recommended only for the experienced.

The twin tourist towns of Fox and Franz Josef are bases for exploring Westland National Park. Activities include visits to the glaciers, numerous walks, glow worm grottoes and Lake Matheson with the View of Views. Guided glacier walks, helicopter rides, scenic flights, horse treks and rafting are the main fee paying activities.

OPTIONS: **SIDE TRIP i** HAAST - JACKSON BAY. A small fishing village 48 km SW of Haast at the end of the road is one of New Zealand's ultimate places in remoteness. A desolate looking place in foul weather, no facilities except a takeaways, a rest area with a shelter and information display.

SIDE TRIP ii FOX - GILLESPIES BEACH. DoC camping (toilets, tables) at north end of beach where old gold workings and a seal colony may be seen. Go 19 km down a no exit gravel road.

15 FRANZ JOSEF - HOKITIKA/GREYMOUTH - WESTPORT.

ROUTE:	SH 6	SH 67
15a) FRANZ JOSEF - GREYMOUTH	174 km	
15b) GREYMOUTH - WESTPORT	101 km	
Side Trip iii WESTPORT - KARAMEA		97 km
Total	275 km	

ALTERNATIVE 15a) MAHINAPUA - HOKITIKA: SH 6 or via Kaniere.
SIDE TRIP 15a) i FORKS - OKARITO. ii HOKITIKA - LAKE KANIERE.
iii HOKITIKA - GOLDSBOROUGH.
15b) i WESTPORT - CAPE FOULWIND ii WESTPORT - KARAMEA on SH 67.
iii DENNISTON INCLINE. iv KARAMEA - COLLINGWOOD on Heaphy Track.
LINK ROAD 15a) HOKITIKA (SH 6) - DONEGALS (SH 73) on Old Chch Highway.

15a FRANZ JOSEF - HOKITIKA - GREYMOUTH. 174km

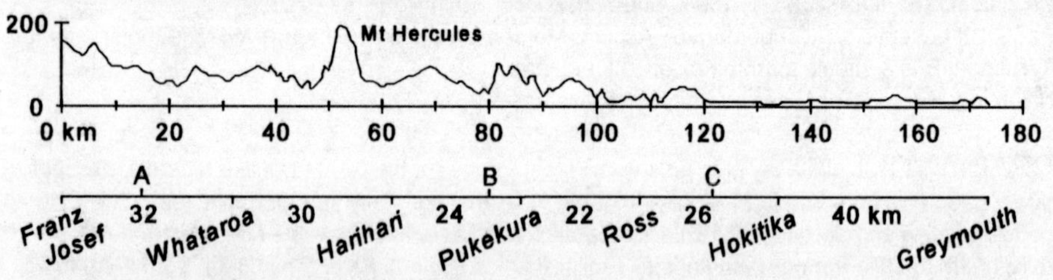

SERVICES: **FRANZ JOSEF GLACIER:** See page 57.
LAKE MAPOURIKA: DoC camping at Otto's Corner (toilet, table). At the north end of the lake is...
MACDONALD'S CREEK: (complete with golden arches), DoC camping (toilet, table, sandflies).
A) FORKS: Lodge/cabins. (2 kms on Okarito Rd). **LAKE WAHOPA:** picnic area.
WHATAROA: Alt 70m, pop 200. Store, tearooms, motel/cabins/tent sites, hotel.
HARIHARI: Alt 90m, pop 600. Food: Store, tearooms, restaurant, pub. Accom: Motel (with cyclists' accom); hotel (also bunkroom & tent sites but no kitchen).
B) LAKE IANTHE: DoC camping (toilets, tables, water). **PUKEKURA:** Tavern/tearooms (incl tent sites, no kitchen); cabins; museum/restaurant. **KAKAPOTAHI:** bkpr hostel.
ROSS: Alt 40m, pop 450. ***i:*** at the museum. Food: Store/tearooms, restaurant, pub.
Accom: 2 motel; 2 hotel (1 with motor camp). **C) LAKE MAHINAPUA:** DoC camping (toilets, water, tables, sandflies) entrance opposite pub (also bkpr accom). Beware: backpacker buses overnight here.
HOKITIKA: Alt 10m, pop 3,300. ***i:*** Cnr Tancred & Hamilton Sts ☎755-6166.
Food: All outlets. Accom: Motor camp; 5 bkpr hostel; 6 motel; 4 hotel. Transport: Bus & shuttle to/from Greymouth, Nelson, Fox & Chch. Bicycle shop. Note: First banks since Wanaka.
KUMARA JUNCTION: Seasonal bkpr hostel (also camp sites) in the old school, open Nov - April.
GREYMOUTH: Alt 10m, pop 13,000. ***i:*** Cnr Mackay & Herbert Sts ☎768-5101.
Food: All outlets. Accom: 2 motor camp; hostel (5 bkpr, 1 YHA); 16 motel; 8 hotel.
Transport: Train to/from Chch. Bus & shuttle to/from Fox, Nelson & Arthur's Pass. Bicycle shops.

GRADIENTS: Gentle gradients for the 32 km from Franz to Whataroa as SH 6 travels past Lake Mapourika, Forks/Okarito turn off, and Lake Wahapo. It continues similar to Whataroa River, then 2 kms of small hills through Whataroa Scenic Reserve and a few kms of flat before reaching Mt Hercules, the last major hill before Greymouth. Narrow and twisting it climbs 4 km to 185m with several places suitable for rests, then a 3 km descent of variable steepness before arriving at Harihari. After Harihari the highway is mostly flat to undulating all the way to Ross, apart from a few kms of rolling hills around Lake Ianthe, Pukekura and Ferguson's Bush. Flat for last 50 km to Greymouth.

ATTRACTIONS: An interesting side trip goes to Okarito, see options below. Mapourika & Wahapo are two pretty lakes between Franz and Whataroa. Seasonal guided tours of the white heron colony leave from Whataroa. Whataroa, Harihari and Ross are small towns servicing the local community and passing tourist traffic, where you might also find the occasional walkway. 20 km after Harihari is the impressive Giant Matai Tree near Lake Ianthe, at over 1,000 years old it's a lumberjack's dream! Pukekura Bush Museum has a monster man-eating (and woman) sandfly above the door, so watch out! Try the local delicacy of possum pie or paté.

Ross owes its origins to gold and has a large working mine behind the town. Here the Honourable Roddy was discovered, at 99oz it is/was the biggest nugget found in NZ. As large as a man's hand it eventually became tableware at Buckingham Palace. After Ross pass Lake Mahinapua and Hotel, made famous by the cheese adverts. Native bush gradually gives way to fertile farmland as Hokitika nears. Hokitika has the first banks since Wanaka. It is famous for greenstone (jade), the raw material is processed locally. Enjoy the road/rail bridges but take care, people have fallen off their bikes.

Grey by name, grey by nature especially on cold wet days, Greymouth is the West Coast's largest town. See the Great Wall of Greymouth, built to stop the Grey River from flooding the town centre. Point Elizabeth walkway and fossicking on the beach are other popular activities. The Brunner Mine historic site is a few kms north on SH 7 where NZ's worst mining disaster occurred in 1896. Combine it with a trip to Blackball and Lake Brunner, where "the fish die of old age".

OPTIONS: **ALTERNATIVE** MAHINAPUA - KANIERE - HOKITIKA. This is 6 km longer than SH6 and has more hills with a significant drop to join Kaniere River. Passes through bush and small settlements. It can be combined with a journey to Lake Kaniere, see Side Trip ii below.
WOODSTOCK: pub. KANIERE: Dairy.

SIDE TRIP i FORKS - OKARITO: DoC camping (toilets, tables, coin showers, sandflies), hostel (2 bkpr, 1 YHA shelter hostel), motel. Once a thriving port town of several thousand is now a small peaceful settlement. Hard to imagine 120 years ago Okarito had 31 hotels and 3 banks. Donovan's Store (now closed and restored) is reputedly the 2nd oldest building on the coast. Take food supplies.

Okarito tends to be drier than at the glaciers being further away from the mountains. Spectacular views of the Southern Alps from Okarito Trig on a 30 minute walk. Explore Okarito Lagoon's white heron colony (seasonal). See the International Airport usually complete with sheep waiting for the next fright! Turn off SH 6 at the Forks 17 km north of Franz Josef going 13 km on a sealed, mostly easy road.

SIDE TRIP ii HOKITIKA - LAKE KANIERE: Hans Bay DoC camping (toilets, water, table) is 18 km inland, a typical bush fringed west coast lake with a few walks, fishing & visit to the nearby Kaniere Gorge is possible.

SIDE TRIP iii to GOLDSBOROUGH: DoC camping (toilets, water, tables) also gold panning, on the site of a gold rush and ghost town, 9 km north of Hokitika on SH 6 and 8 km inland. It can also be used as a link road to/from Chch joining SH 73 at Dillmanstown. Some gravel but easier than....

LINK ROAD HOKITIKA - DONEGALS on Old Chch Highway, 8 km north of Hokitika turn off SH 6, going right on north bank Arahura River and travel 22½ km. Mostly easy going and sealed except at the eastern end when encountering a steep downhill with loose and deep gravel.

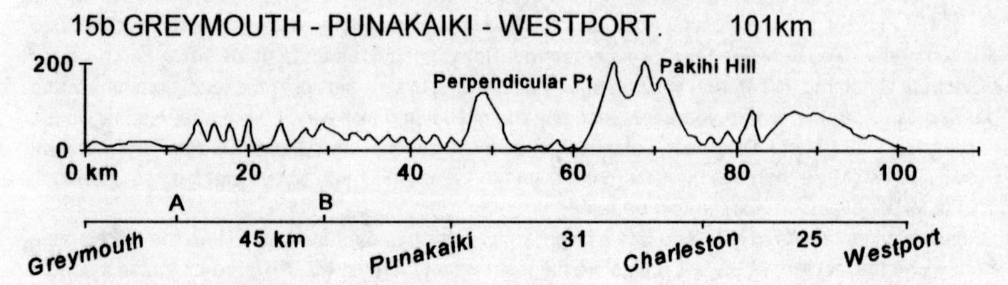

SERVICES: **GREYMOUTH:** See previous section.
RUNANGA: Alt 40m. Store/takeaways, pub, bkpr hostel.
A) RAPAHOE: Motor camp. **9 MILE CREEK:** picnic area. **13 MILE CREEK:** picnic areas.
B) BARRYTOWN: Alt 50m, pop 15. Hotel (also bkpr accom & takeaways).
PUNAKAIKI: Alt 30m, pop 40. ***i:*** DoC, Main Rd ☎731-1895. Food: Tearooms/takeaways, dairy. Accom: Motor camp; 2 bkpr hostel; 2 motel; hotel. **PERPENDICULAR Pt:** picnic area.
CHARLESTON: Alt 50m, pop 100. Pub, motor camp/dairy/takeaways; bkpr hostel (8 km N); motel.
WESTPORT: Alt 10m, pop 4,500. ***i:*** 1 Brougham St ☎789-6658. Food: All outlets.
Accom: 2 motor camp (1 at beach 6 km from Westport); hostel (3 bkpr, 1 YHA); 6 motel; 4 hotel.
Transport: Bus & shuttle to/from Nelson, Chch, Greymouth & Karamea. Bicycle shops.

GRADIENTS: Fairly easy for the first 12 km, passing through Runanga until reaching the coast at Rapahoe. After Rapahoe SH 6 has some fairly long climbs & descents for 14 km as it negotiates several bluffs. At Barker's Creek the highway heads inland and gradients become easy again for 19 km, re-joining the coast at Punakaiki.

After Punakaiki undulations continue along the coast for the next 15 km, apart from a steep 2 km climb and similar 2 km drop to cross the bluffs of Perpendicular Pt. 4 km north of Fox River start three steep hills of variable length & height in 11 km, reaching 200m and ending 1 km before Charleston. Mostly undulates from there to Westport apart from Costello Hill.

ATTRACTIONS: Runanga is a small coal mining town at the southern end of the Paparoa Range overlooked by an unusually named Old Baldy hill! The bluffs and coastal scenes north of Rapahoe and around Punakaiki are impressive. The Croesus Track at Barrytown goes over the hills to Blackball.

Punakaiki is the base for exploring Paparoa National Park. Nearby are the Pancake Rocks and blowholes, black petrel colony, canoe trips, caving and several walks. Limestone cliffs and headlands dominate the scene. Perpendicular Pt is aptly named! The tiny settlement of Charleston was yet another prosperous gold mining town, now a sleepy settlement. Westport is the second largest town of the West Coast and owes its existence to coal, hence the Coaltown Museum. Nearby Cape Foulwind & Tauranga Bay has a seal colony.

OPTIONS: SIDE TRIP i WESTPORT - CAPE FOULWIND & TAURANGA BAY seal colony, 18 km west of Westport via Carters Beach and cement works on an easy undulating road. There is a car park & shelter at the start of the walkway. Named by Capt Cook after being caught in unpleasant weather and currents, not because of the smell from below!

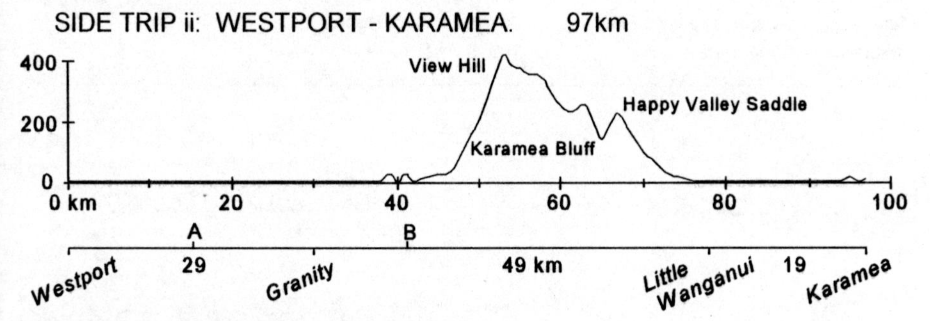

SERVICES: **WESTPORT:** See previous page.
A) WAIMANGAROA: Alt 20m, pub, store. **GRANITY:** Pub, store/takeaways.
NGAKAWAU/HECTOR: store, pub, bkper hostel. **MOKIHINUI:** Store.
B) WAIMARIE: Pub, domain motor camp. **SEDDONVILLE:** Store, pub, domain motor camp, hotel.
LITTLE WANGANUI: Alt 10m. Hotel (also bkpr accom).
KARAMEA: Alt 10m. ***i:*** Waverley St ☎782-6820. Food: All outlets except supermarket.
Accom: Domain camping/bunkhouse; motor camp (3 km S); bkpr hostel; motel; hotel.
Transport: Bus to Westport (Mon to Fri).

GRADIENTS: SH 67 is mostly flat all the way to Karamea, apart from the occasional small hill and Karamea Bluff. This comprises mainly of two long ups & downs of variable length and steepness that cross View Hill Saddle (420m) & Happy Valley Saddle (283m) on the way to Little Wanganui. An easy 16 km of alternating seal/gravel road goes from Karamea to Kohaihai and start of the Heaphy Track.

ATTRACTIONS: Travel up the coast passing small settlements on the way. Granity, Ngakawau & Hector are the base villages for open cast coal mines on the plateau above. Seddonville is a small settlement 5 km off the highway in a pleasant setting with a few local walks. Karamea Bluff offers fine views of the surrounding area and cuts off Karamea from civiisation. Little Wanganui is a small settlement and western access point of the Wangapeka Track. Karamea is a quiet, sprawling village with plenty of beautiful natural features dotting the area. Explore Kahurangi, NZ's newest National Park.

OPTIONS: **SIDE TRIP iii** WAIMANGAROA - DENNISTON INCLINE HISTORIC RESERVE.
9 km inland up a steep narrow winding road is the disused railway line on a 1:1 hill. It once hauled coal down from mines high on the Rochford Plateau 600 m ASL. Amazing coastal views from the top complete with a walkway, information displays, remnants of the railway, coal mine and ghost town.

SIDE TRIP iv KARAMEA - KOHAIHAI: DoC camping (toilets, shelter, water, tables) 16 km N of Karamea. The south end of the HEAPHY TRACK a DoC Great Walk taking trampers to Golden Bay through Kahurangi National Park. Now closed to mountain bikes.

NORTH

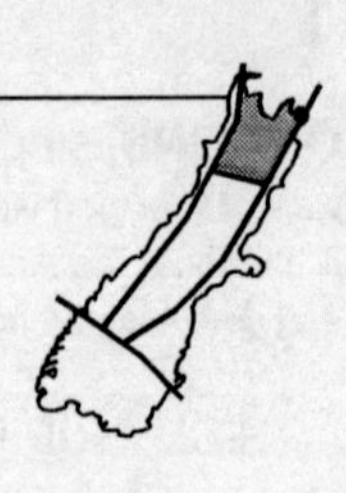

HIGHLIGHTS (not in any order of preference)

Nelson City & Tasman Bay
Nelson Lakes National Park
Able Tasman National Park
Marlborough Sounds Maritime Park
Kahurangi National Park
Golden Bay & Farewell Spit
Takaka Hill & Harwoods Hole
Murchison & Buller Gorge
Motueka River Road
Rainbow Track

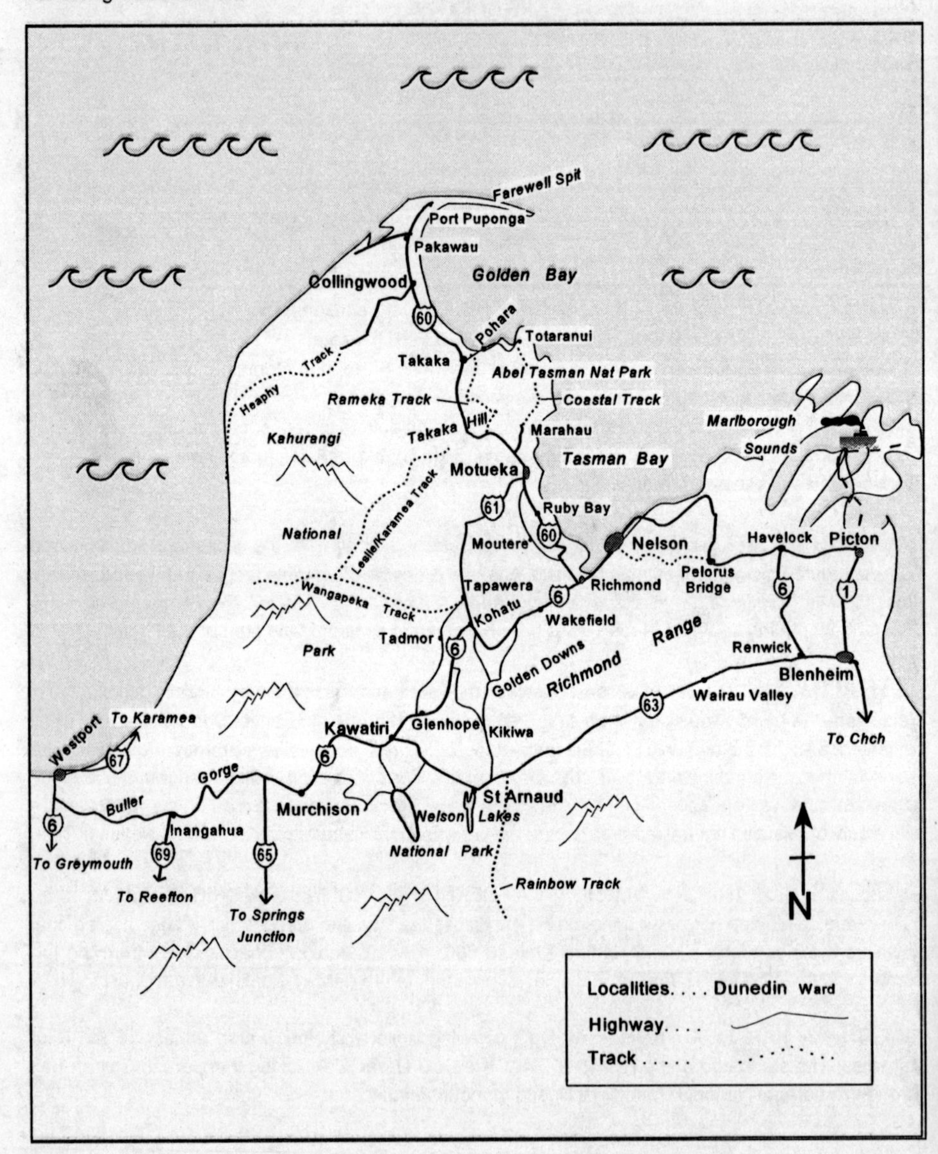

16 WESTPORT - KAWATIRI JUNCTION - NELSON.

ROUTE:	SH 6	Various roads
16a) WESTPORT - MURCHISON - KAWATIRI JUNCT	133 km	
16b) KAWATIRI JUNCT - KOHATU - NELSON	92 km*	
link iii KAWATIRI JUNCT - ST ARNAUD - MOTUEKA		129 km*
link iv KAWATIRI JUNCT - ST ARNAUD - BLENHEIM	_____	127 km
Total	225 km	

* Note: Beware logging trucks in and around forest plantations.

ALTERNATIVE 16b) KAWATIRI JUNCTION - NELSON. The shorter, busier SH 6 over Hope Saddle or the quieter more interesting route via St Arnaud. Both meet at Belgrove. Add 23 km if taking this alternative (see 16a Link Road iii (next page) as far as Golden Downs, near Kohatu).

LINK ROAD 16a) i INANGAHUA (SH 6) - REEFTON (SH 7) on SH 69. (Page 64).
ii MURCHISON (SH 6) - SPRINGS JUNCTION (SH 7) on SH 65. (Page 64).
iii KAWATIRI JUNCTION - ST ARNAUD - MOTUEKA on various highways. (Page 64).
16b) iv ST ARNAUD - BLENHEIM (SH 1) on SH 63. (Page 65).
v St ARNAUD (SH 63) - RAINBOW TRACK - HANMER SPRINGS (SH 7). (Page 27).
vi MOTUEKA - NELSON (Page 68).

16a WESTPORT - MURCHISON - KAWATIRI JUNCTION. 133km

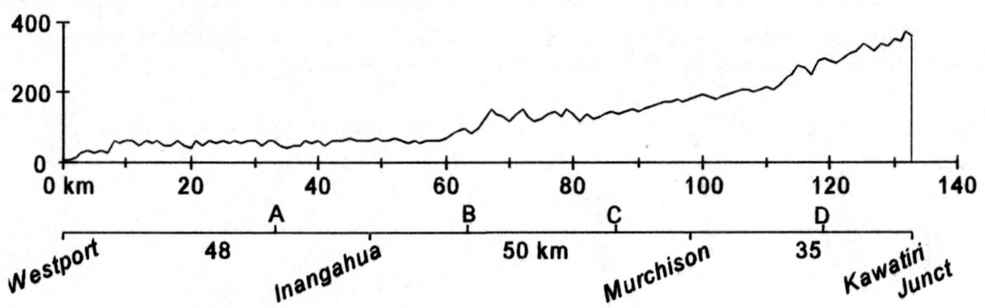

SERVICES: **WESTPORT:** See page 60. **A) BERLINS:** Alt 48m, pub/tearooms/bkpr hostel.
INANGAHUA JUNCTION: Alt 60m, pop 50. Store.
B) LYELL: Alt 100m. DoC camping (toilets, water, table). **C) JUNCTION SH6/65:** picnic area.
MURCHISON: Alt 180m, pop 600. ***i:*** Main Road, ☎523-9350 (seasonal).
Food: Tearooms, takeaways, store, restaurant. Accom: Motor camp (2 km N); cabins; bkpr hostel; 2 motel; hotel. Transport: Bus to Greymouth, Westport, Nelson & Chch. **MANGLES RIVER:** picnic area.
D) OWEN RIVER: Alt 260m. Hotel/motel, Domain camping (toilets, water, coin shower, shelter).
GOWAN BRIDGE: Motor camp (seasonal) picnic area.
KAWATIRI JUNCTION: Alt 360m, picnic area (shelter, toilet, table, water).

GRADIENTS: Mostly flat for the first 11 km from Westport until joining the Buller River and entering the Buller Gorge. High, steep, bush-clad walls dominate most of the next 133 km as the road rolls and undulates up-stream to Kawatiri Junction. The only exceptions being flatter sections around Berlins, Inangahua Junction and Murchison where the hills fall back temporarily leaving broad open valleys.

ATTRACTIONS: The Buller River has a variety of interesting sights for the passing cyclist. Fern Arch Half Bridge, Hawk's Crag, Berlins & Inangahua in the lower gorge. Lyell Historic Reserve, (now a ghost town), Buller Gorge Swingbridge, Ariki Falls, Old Man Mountain & Murchison township in the Upper Buller Gorge.

At Murchison there is an interesting museum and nearby is NZ's oldest hydro power scheme. Inangahua (1968) and Murchison (1929) suffered devastating earthquakes with many scars on the hillsides as reminders of the unstable nature of the area. An ambitious railway project intending to go from Nelson to Westport only made it to Kawatiri Junction, has long since closed. See the tunnel.

OPTIONS: **LINK ROAD i** INANGAHUA JUNCTION - REEFTON is an easy 34 km climb on SH 69 alongside Inangahua River, INANGAHUA BRIDGE: bkpr hostel, for beyond Reefton see page 28.

LINK ROAD ii MURCHISON - SHENANDOAH SADDLE - SPRINGS JUNCTION on SH 65. 83 km
The highway rolls and undulates upstream alongside the Maruia River passing . . .
MARUIA FALLS: picnic area (tables), 10 km S of SH 6/65 junction. This is the main attraction of SH 65, being formed in only 1929 as a result of the earthquake diverting the river from its normal course. 13 km south of Maruia Falls is Moonlight (expensive lodge). After leaving limestone country of the Buller Gorge enter the podocarp forests of Victoria Forest Park. A steady 6½ km climb to romantically named SHENANDOAH SADDLE (500m) is followed by a 6½ km descent, the middle part around Frog Flat (Burnbrae) being very gentle.

SH 65 then alternates between undulating and rolling until Rapahancock Stream. Braided river flats and farms in the valley bottom, native forests on the mountainsides most of the way to Springs Junction. Almost flat for much of the 18 km from MARUIA SETTLEMENT (tearooms, motel) (the store//bkpr hostel hasn't reopened) to Springs Junction. See for onward travel (pages 27/28).

16a LINK iii: KAWATIRI JUNCT - ST ARNAUD - MOTUEKA. 129km

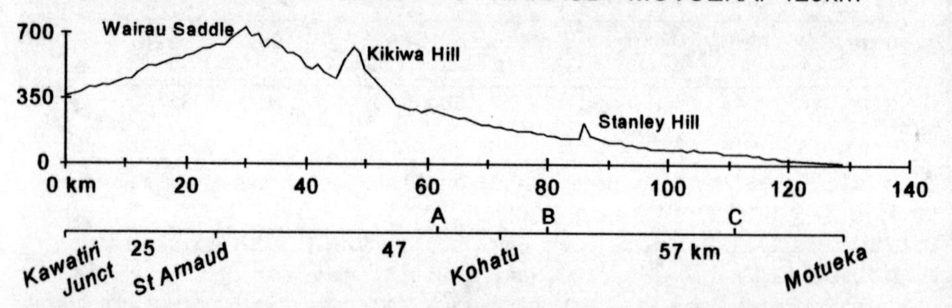

SERVICES: **KAWATIRI JUNCTION:** Alt 360m, DoC camping (toilet, shelter, table, water). Cyclists hostel at Glenhope, 9km up SH 6. See page 66 for more details.

St ARNAUD: Alt 630m, pop 200. ***i:*** DoC ☎521-1806. Food: Store/takeaways, restaurant.
Accom: DoC camping (shelter, water, tables, coin showers, no cabins); bkpr hostel; hotel.
Transport: Bus to/from Blenheim & Greymouth. Shuttle to/from Nelson.

A) GOLDEN DOWNS: picnic area. **KOHATU:** Alt 190m, pub.

B) TAPAWERA: Alt 150m, pop 450. Takeaways, store, pub, motor camp.

C) NGATIMOTI: Alt 60m. Dairy. **MOTUEKA:** See page 68.

GRADIENTS: At Kawatiri Junction join SH 63 gradually climbing most of the 25 km to St. Arnaud, with a 1 km steeper section part way. After St Arnaud continue to climb for 5 km and go left to Tophouse & Golden Downs. One steep dip and climb near Tophouse and a steep climb just after Kikiwa, otherwise mostly variable downhill to Golden Downs.

Note 1: Those wanting to avoid Kikiwa Hill after Kikiwa should go left at the junction to Korere, then right on SH 6 to Kohatu and left to Motueka. This way is 4 km longer than through Golden Downs.

Note 2: Alternative to SH 6 to Nelson: Go right at Golden Downs. There's a long climb and drop over Wai-iti Saddle (429m) otherwise nothing too strenuous. Rejoin SH 6 at Belgrove. See 16b below for Belgrove to Nelson. This route via St Arnaud is 23 km longer than SH 6.

Gentle down from Golden Downs through Kohatu until 5 km after Tapawera. Then a steep 1½ km climb to the top of Stanley Hill (244m) and an equally steep and winding 2 km descent on the other side. The highway then rejoins and meanders downstream alongside the Motueka River for most of the way to Motueka, the gradients become more gentle as the coast nears.

ATTRACTIONS: Nelson Lakes National Park is one of the quieter parks with the main features being St Arnaud Village, Mt Robert, Lakes Rotoiti & Rotoroa. Tramping, fishing, climbing and skiing are the most popular pastimes in and around the park. Tophouse was once a historic hotel is now a guest house. Travel through some of the 30,000 hectares of the Golden Downs Forest, the second biggest plantation in NZ. Tapawera is the main settlement of the Upper Motueka Valley, gain access to Kahurangi National Park and the eastern end of the Wangapeka Track. Follow the Motueka River down to Motueka, an important hop and fruit growing area as well as a popular retirement and holiday centre. This is the gateway to Golden Bay and closest settlement to Abel Tasman National Park.

OPTIONS: **LINK ROAD iv** ST ARNAUD - BLENHEIM on SH 63. Distance 102 km.
See page 67 for details.

LINK ROAD v St ARNAUD (SH 63) - RAINBOW TRACK - HANMER SPRINGS (SH 7) 130 km.
Take the turn-off to Rainbow Skifield. See page 27 for details.

16b KAWATIRI JUNCTION - HOPE SADDLE - NELSON. 92km

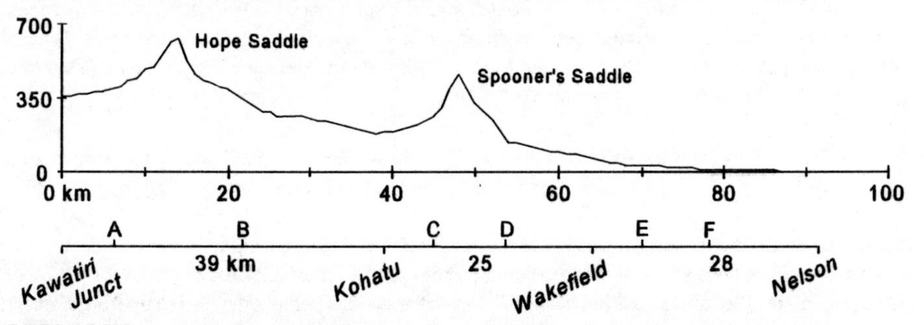

SERVICES: **KAWATIRI JUNCTION:** Alt 360m, DoC camping (shelter, toilet, table, water).
A) GLENHOPE: Cyclists farm hostel (see next page for details).
HOPE SADDLE: picnic area (toilet, table, shelter).
B) CLARKE VALLEY: Recreational Reserve, DoC camping (toilet, water, table).
MOTUPIKO: Christian camp (no cabins, minimum "donation"). **KOHATU:** Alt 190m, pub.

C) NORRIS GULLY: Rec Res. DoC camping (toilet, water, table). **D) BELGROVE:** Alt 135m Pub. **WAKEFIELD:** Alt 60m, pop 850. Store, tearooms, pub. **E) BRIGHTWATER:** Alt 30m Store, pub. **F) RICHMOND:** Alt 20m, pop 7,000. ***i:*** Gladstone Rd (SH 6) ☎544-4793. Food: All outlets. Accom: Motor camp; 5 motel; 4 hotel. Bicycle shop. **NELSON:** See next section.

HU-HA BIKEPACKERS
State Highway 6, RD2 Glenhope.
Hosts: Sam Midgely and Jo Meek
9 km north of Kawatiri Junction.
Telephone: (03)548-2707, Fax: (03)548-2804.
Email: smidgley@ihug.co.nz
Website: paradise-press.co.nz/accom.html
Accommodation: 1 x 4 bunk room $23.00pp,
1 double room $28.00pp,
1 ensuite double $33.00pp, tent sites $14.00pp.
($3.00 less for BBH Card holders)
Special Features: Spacious Lounge.
Full kitchen facilities. Basic food supplies.
On 600 hectacre sheep, cattle, goat and pig farm.
Mountain biking opportunities available on farm and in surrounding forest.

Distances from Glenhope to...
Kawatiri Junction: 9 km (junct SH63 & SH6.)
St Arnaud (Nelson Lakes): 31 km
Motueka: 80 km — Murchison: 41 km
Nelson: 80 km — Westport: 139 km

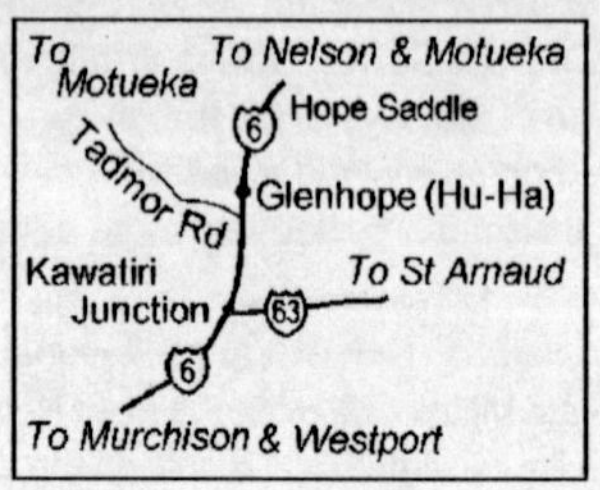

GRADIENTS: On leaving Kawatiri Junction, SH 6 climbs gradually to Hope Saddle (635m) becoming steeper for the last few km as it nears the top. A very steep winding descent for 2 km is followed by undulations with a downward trend to Korere. At Korere the valley widens with easy gradients through Kohatu until Norris Stream where the highway starts its ascent to Spooners Saddle (464m), the last 1½ km is quite steep and winding. This is followed by a long steady steep to quite steep descent of 300m in 6½ km to Belgrove. Gentle down from Belgrove through Wakefield to Richmond and then flat into Nelson. Richmond & Stoke are becoming part of Nelson with considerable urban traffic flows. Use one of the cycle paths into Nelson (see page 70).

ATTRACTIONS: Panoramic views from Hope and Spooners Saddles, travel through part of the huge Golden Downs Plantation, the second largest exotic forest in NZ. Lord Rutherford "the father of nuclear physics" had his first schooling at Foxhill and at Brightwater, his birthplace, has a memorial showing events in his life. In between is the small village of Wakefield with St John's, the South Island's oldest surviving church built in 1846 and the Pigeon Valley Steam Museum. Pass many small farms, orchards and tiny settlements on the way to Nelson.

OPTIONS: **ALTERNATIVE** KAWATIRI JUNCTION - ST ARNAUD - NELSON. This scenic route is 23 km longer than SH 6. See 16a Link Road iii above to Golden Downs, near Kohatu (page 64/65).

LINK ROAD GLENHOPE (SH 6) - TADMOR - TAPAWERA (SH 61). Distance: 40 km.

If you plan to miss Nelson Lakes and go direct to/from Abel Tasman/Golden Bay then try this quiet, partly gravel route. The turn-off is 2 km down SH 6 from the cyclists hostel and 7½ km up from Kawatiri Junction. It follows the route of the old railway line that went through to Kawatiri Junction. Starts with a moderate climb to Tadmor Saddle then a moderate descent followed by a mostly undulating downhill all the way to Tapawera (see page 64). No services.

16b LINK iv: KAWATIRI JUNCTION - St ARNAUD - BLENHEIM. 127km

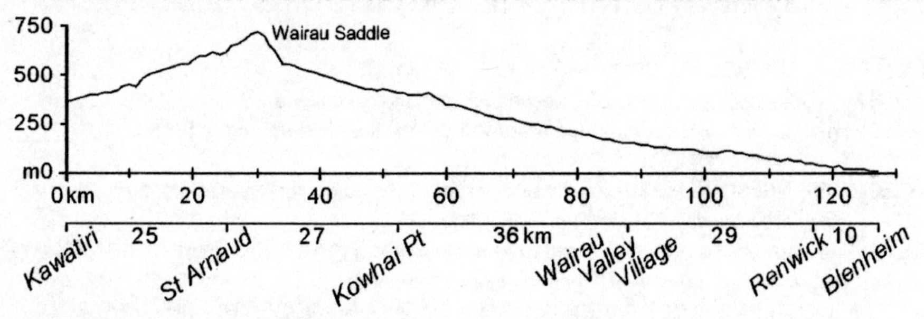

SERVICES: **KAWATIRI JUNCTION:** Alt 360m, DoC camping (toilet, shelter, table, water). Cyclists hostel at Glenhope, 9km up SH 6. See page 66 for more details.
St ARNAUD: Alt 630m, pop 200. *i:* DoC ☎521-1806. Food: Store/takeaways, restaurant. Accom: DoC camping (shelter, water, tables, coin showers, no cabins); bkpr hostel; hotel. Transport: Bus to/from Blenheim & Greymouth. Shuttle to/from Nelson.
KOWHAI Pt: Alt 410m, DoC camping (toilet, water, table).
WAIRAU VALLEY VILLAGE: Alt 160m, Hotel (also small shop & camping, no kitchen).
RENWICK: Alt; 30m, Supermarket, takeaways/tearooms, dairy, bkpr hostel, motel, pub.
BLENHEIM: See page 11 for onward travel.

GRADIENTS: At Kawatiri Junction join SH 63, gradually climbing most of the 25 km to St. Arnaud, with a 1 km steeper section part way. After St Arnaud the road continues to climb for 5 km, passing the turn off to Nelson & Tophouse before reaching the summit (727m). Then starts a sometimes steep descent for 6 km as SH 63 passes through 6 Mile Scenic Reserve, easing on joining Wairau River. Then follows a fairly steep descent to the Wash Bridge across the Wairau River.

Apart from a few undulations and bends between Wash Bridge and Branch River, SH 63 tracks gently downhill with the hills slowly falling back for most of the way to the junction with SH 6 at Renwick. The last 10 km to Blenheim are flat except one hump at The Fairhall Diversion. To bypass Blenheim, go north onto SH 6 at Renwick for 3 km then go right via Rapaura to Spring Creek and left on SH 1 towards Picton. Mostly easy gradients from Blenheim to Picton.

ATTRACTIONS: Nelson Lakes is one of the quieter national parks with the main features being St Arnaud Village, Mt Robert, and lakes Rotoiti & Rotoroa. Tramping, fishing, climbing and skiing are the most popular pastimes in and around the park. Isolated sheep stations and forest plantations predominate in the Wairau Valley. To the north see Red Hill which over the years has drifted north from Fiordland and is now at the western edge of Mt Richmond Forest Park.

Usually very quiet. The tiny Wairau Valley Village is the only settlement in the Wairau Valley and is being transformed by palatial homes on lifestyle blocks. Almost all the orchards around Renwick and Blenheim have mostly been replaced with vineyards.

OPTIONS: RAINBOW TRACK link road to Hanmer Springs. See page 27.

17 NELSON - MOTUEKA - COLLINGWOOD (Golden Bay).

ROUTE: NELSON - COLLINGWOOD 133 km on SH 60

* Add 6 km if going via Upper Moutere, between Richmond & Motueka.

** Add 25 km if going on to Port Puponga (Farewell Spit) at the northern end of SH 60.

ALTERNATIVE NELSON - MOTUEKA. The easier, busy SH 60 or more interesting, hilly Upper Moutere Highway. This is 6 km longer than SH 60.

SIDE TRIP i RIWAKA - MARAHAU (S end of Abel Tasman). ii UPPER TAKAKA - COBB VALLEY. iii TAKAKA - TOTARANUI (N end of Abel Tasman). iv COLLINGWOOD - FAREWELL SPIT. v COLLINGWOOD - HEAPHY TRACK.

LINK ROAD MOTUEKA - KOHATU - St ARNAUD on SH 61. See page 64.

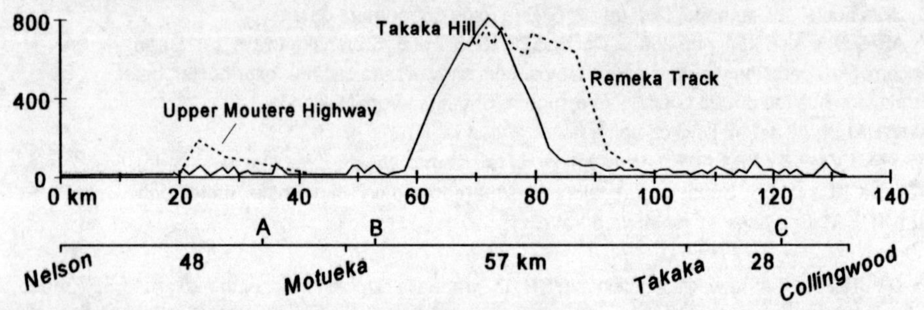

SERVICES: **NELSON:** See page 70-71. **MAPUA:** Store, tearooms. Motor camp (clothes optional!).

A) RUBY BAY: Store, domain camping (caretaker, no cabins).

MOTUEKA: Alt 30m, pop 5,000. ***i:*** *236 High St ☎528-6543, or *DoC, Cnr High & King Edward Sts ☎528-9117 for tramping. Food: All outlets. Accom: 2 motor camp; 5 bkpr hostel; 6 motel; hotel. Bicycle shop. Transport: Bus & shuttles to/from Nelson, Abel Tasman National Park & Golden Bay.

B) RIWAKA: Dairy/takeaways, pub. **SUMMIT:** 810m, picnic area.

TAKAKA: Alt 30m, pop 1300. ***i:*** Willow St ☎525-9136. Food: All outlets (supermarket open 5½ days). Accom: 5 bkpr hostel; 2 motel; 2 hotel. Bicycle shop. Transport: Bus to/from Collingwood, Heaphy Track, Totaranui (Abel Tasman NP) & Nelson. **TAKAKA RIVER:** Informal camping.

C) ONEKAKA:(16 km NW of Takaka) Beach farm hostel (seasonal).

TUKURUA BEACH: (18km NW of Takaka) Motor camp.

COLLINGWOOD: pop 200. Food: Store, tearooms, pub. Accom: Motor camp; bkpr hostel; 2 motel.

GRADIENTS: Leave Nelson either via Rocks Rd and Tahunanui, or the Railway Reserve cycle track (see map). At Richmond go right on SH 60. It conitnues flat along SH 60 to Motueka except for rolling hills between Moutere and Mapua turn-offs and a hill at the north end of Ruby Bay.

SH 60 to Golden Bay continues mostly flat to Riwaka then 2 km after the bridge it climbs for 11 km, often steep & winding to the Ngarua Caves. A short dip and rise follow before reaching the saddle (810m). A long and sometimes steep descent begins with several switch-backs until Upper Takaka. Easy gradients track downhill from there for most of the 22 km to Takaka. The 28 km to Collingwood undulates and rolls with the occasional steeper hill. Alternatively near the top of Takaka Hill take the gravel, sometimes steep Canaan Road to Harwood's Hole and join Rameka Track to Takaka. There's some bush bashing so only recommended for lightly ladened bikes.

ATTRACTIONS: Several orchards and vineyards dot the highway between Nelson and Motueka, some with roadside stalls from which to sample fresh fruit in season. Near Motueka is the seaside holiday village of Kaiteriteri, reputedly the prettiest beach in NZ, the population explodes during summer school holidays. Marahau has Abel Tasman National Park & interestingly named Astrolabe Roadstead on the doorstep with tramping, diving and sea kayaking opportunities. Abel Tasman is one of the most popular national parks and usually very crowded during summer. The Coastal Track, a DoC Great Walk, passes numerous bays & white sandy beaches with bush clad hills as a backdrop. 7 km off SH 60 is the source of Riwaka River as it appears from a cave, a nice place to cool off on a hot day.

Limestone caves and sinkholes are features of Takaka Hill, giving it a weird landscape. The area is popular for caving. Harwood's Hole at 183m deep and 50m wide is said to be the largest in the Southern Hemisphere. If going here, try the sometimes rough and steep Rameka Track down to Takaka (only for lightly loaded bikes). One suggestion is to cycle to Takaka and kayak back.

Golden Bay, cut off from civilization by Takaka Hill, is a favourite place of holiday makers, hermits, alternative lifestylers and beached whales. Quiet sandy beaches abound from where numerous watery pastimes are pursued. Access to Totaranui and the northern end of Abel Tasman National Park is from Takaka. 7 km from Takaka is Waikoropupu Springs, the largest fresh water spring in NZ with large volumes of remarkably clear water gushing from a hole in the ground. Collingwood is in an idyllic setting, like so many places here. The eastern end of the Heaphy Track (a DoC Great Walk) starts 35 km inland. Nearby Farewell Spit has a wildlife sanctuary and is the top of the Mainland.

OPTIONS: **ALTERNATIVE** NELSON - MOTUEKA on UPPER MOUTERE HIGHWAY.
After Appleby Bridge leave SH 60 and go left onto Golden Hills Rd. The first few km have gentle gradients, then climb for 3 km passing REDWOOD VALLEY arriving at Moutere Saddle (183m). The road descends 1½ km then undulates down for 3½ km.
UPPER MOUTERE: Store, vineyards. The historic St Paul's Lutheran Church is a visible reminder of the first German settlement in NZ. Becomes mostly flat the rest of the way to Motueka.
At LOWER MOUTERE: Store, Riverside Community (hostel & camping) is one of the oldest surviving communes in NZ, established about 1941 by a Christian pacifist group, visitors welcome. Nearby tame eels can be seen. This route is 6 km longer than SH 60.

SIDE TRIP i RIWAKA - MARAHAU Distance 15 km via KAITERITERI (takeaways/motor camp, motel) and the coast, or 12 km by the inland route, both are.hilly, narrow and winding and arrive at MARAHAU: (takeaways, motor camp, bkpr hostel) is at the southern entrance of Abel Tasman National Park.

SIDE TRIP ii UPPER TAKAKA - COBB VALLEY RESERVOIR Turn west from Upper Takaka travelling through gentle valley pasturelands. After crossing Takaka River, the road narrows, twisting with moderate climbs as it follows the river into the heart of Kahurangi National Park, some gravel. Surrounded by lush native forests and mountain views galore. The road ends near Trilobite Hut on the western edge of the reservoir. Serious tramping starts here (no bikes).

SIDE TRIP iii TAKAKA - TOTARANUI. Distance 32 km east On the way to Totaranui at the northern end of Abel Tasman National Park go past . . . CLIFTON RESERVE: (The Grove) 8km E of Takaka a mystical rata forest grows on top of huge limestone outcrops, then . . .
POHARA BEACH: (10 km from Takaka). Dairy, restaurant; beach camp; bkpr hostel; motel 5.
TASMAN MEMORIAL (13 km) commemorates the first visit to NZ by Europeans in 1642 and
LIGAR BAY (13km) Toilets. A good wading beach with penguins, dolphins but beware of stingrays.
TATA BEACH (15 km) Motel. Beyond Tata Beach the road becomes, narrow, steep, rolling and twisting but very scenic. Gravel starts at Wainui Bay (18km), climbing steeply to 300m with a steep descent before arriving at TOTARANUI: *i:* DoC ☎528-8083. Motor camp (no cabins) bookings essential before proceeding during summer school holidays.

SIDE TRIP iv COLLINGWOOD - PAKAWAU (13 km N on SH 60) Motor camp (small store); bkpr hostel; restaurant. PORT PUPONGA (25 km) motor camp, seasonal bkpr hostel. Visit the farm park and wildlife sanctuary (seasonal visitor centre and tearooms).

A detour goes to WHARARIKI BEACH (8 km W of Puponga), gravel with some moderate climbs. A steep northern side road at about 4 km leads to CAPE FAREWELL, the South Island's most northern point. At the end of the main road at WHARARIKI, a short tramp leads to sandstone arches and caves.

SIDE TRIP v COLLINGWOOD - BAINHAM and the HEAPHY TRACK going through Kahurangi National Park to reach Karamea and the West Coast. Closed to mountain bikers.

18 NELSON.

DIRECTIONS: **WEST**: From WESTPORT & GOLDEN BAY: Get a Nelson Information Centre map from the Richmond Information Centre on Gladstone Road, Richmond.

Shortly after Richmond on the seaward side of the new Richmond Deviation is a cycle path that goes all the way to the Happy Lawyer Hotel. Go left a short distance on Songer St and right to rejoin the cycle path to the airport. Beyond the airport go straight on Bolt Road, left onto Parker's Road, right onto Golf Road and straight along Beach Road. Bear left onto Rocks Road cycle path going all the way to the city.

Alternatively there is the Railway Reserve cycle path that uses an old rail corridor going between Saxton Road on the Richmond side of Stoke and St Vincent/Halifax Sts. It runs parallel to Waimea and Stoke Main Roads and is more hilly than Rocks Road route, but it avoids other traffiic.

NORTH: To PICTON: Go north along Trafalgar St to the junction, bear right onto Queen Elizabeth Drive. The first 12 km on leaving Nelson are mostly flat.

SERVICES: **NELSON/STOKE:** Altitude 20m, population 40,000.
i: Cnr Trafalgar & Halifax Sts ☎548-2304. Food: Many choices of all types of outlets.
Accom: 4 motor camp; hostel (15 bkpr, 1 YHA); lots motel; many hotel. Bicycle shops.
Transport: Bus & shuttles to/from Christchurch, Picton, West Coast, Golden Bay & Nelson Lakes.

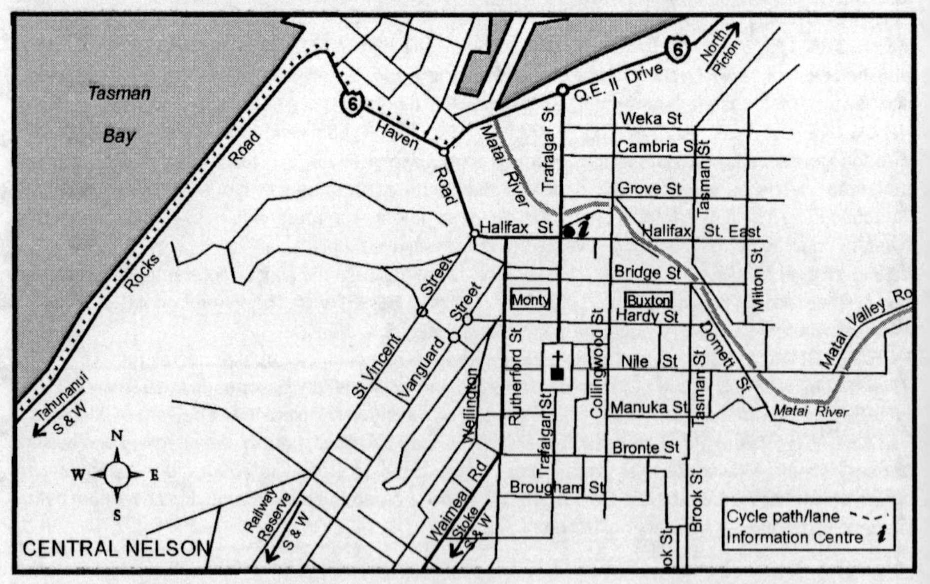

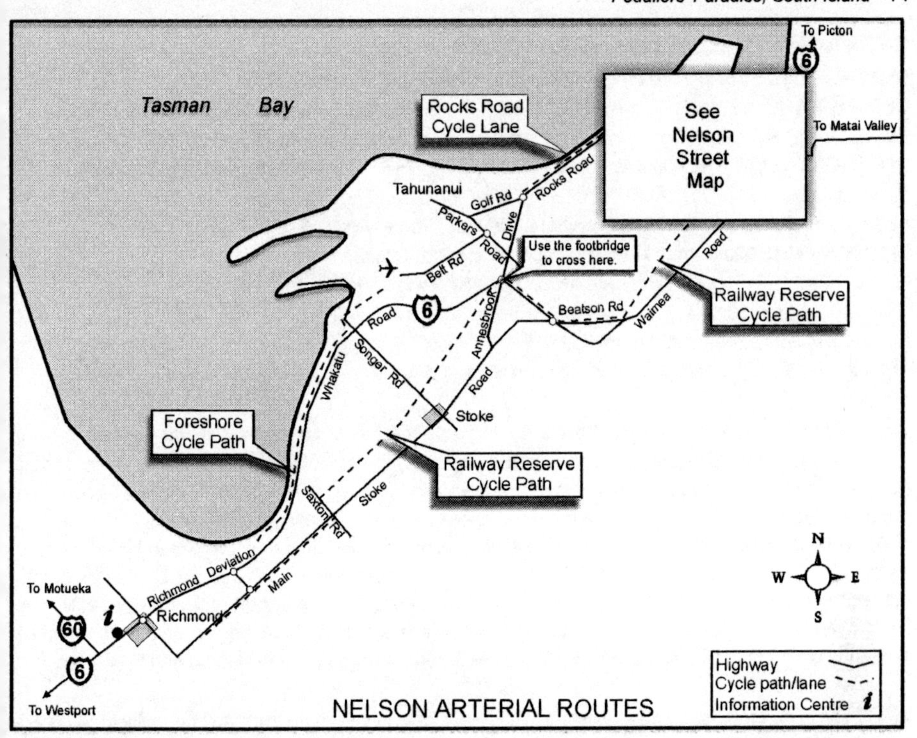

ATTRACTIONS: The first "big" city since the West Coast or last if heading there. After an uncertain beginning Nelson has blossomed into a prosperous community. Competes with Blenheim for the sunniest place in NZ. The largest city & port of the region with all the entertainments, activities and services expected in a modern city, although at the moment I can't remember any of them. Nelson is often used as a base for exploring Abel Tasman National Park.

19 NELSON - PICTON.

ROUTE: NELSON - PICTON 109 km on SH 6. and Queen Charlotte Sound.

ALTERNATIVE NELSON - PELORUS BRIDGE via Mangatapu Saddle. For the brave.

SIDE TRIP To MARLBOROUGH SOUNDS MARITIME PARK from:

i RAI VALLEY (by road) & HAVELOCK (by boat). ii LINKWATER (by gravel road).

LINK ROAD HAVELOCK - BLENHEIM on SH 6.

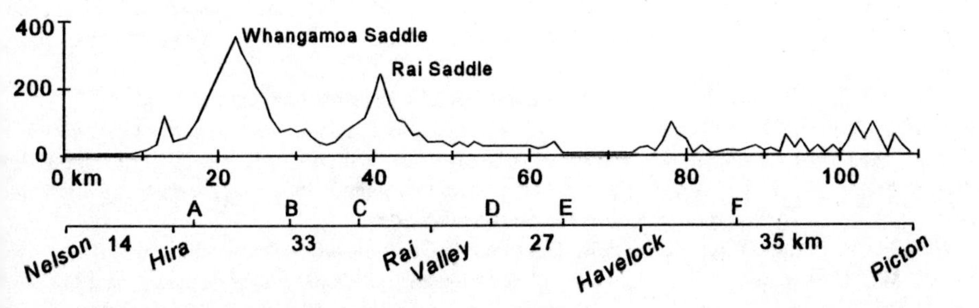

SERVICES: **NELSON:** See pages 70-71. **HIRA:** Store/tearooms.
A) HIRA FOREST: picnic area. **B) GRAHAM STREAM:** picnic area (toilet).
C) COLLINS VALLEY: picnic area. **RAI VILLAGE:** Alt 50m, pop 200. Store/tearooms, bkpr hostel.
D) PELORUS BRIDGE: Tearooms/motor camp.
E) CANVASTOWN: Pop 100. Motor camp (8 km S off SH 6); hotel (also small shop & tent sites).
HAVELOCK: Alt 20m, pop 400. Food: Store, tearooms, restaurant, pub, mussel factory.
Accom: 2 motor camp (1 is 7 km S on SH 6); hostel (1 bkpr 9km E, 1 YHA); motel; hotel.
F) LINKWATER: Store, motor camp (2km on Kenepuru Road).
THE GROVE: motel (also camping). **MOMORANGI BAY:** Motor camp.
PICTON: Altitude 10m, population 4,000. ***i:*** Foreshore ☎573-7477. Food: All outlets.
Accom: 5 motor Camp; hostel (6 bkpr, 1 YHA); 11 motel; 4 hotel. Transport: Ferry to/from Wellington. Train to/from Chch. Buses & shuttles to/from Nelson & Chch.

GRADIENTS: The first 12 km out of Nelson are mostly flat as SH 6 runs alongside Tasman Bay for 9 km with another flat 3 km heading inland to the bottom of the first of three hills. Gentle Annie Saddle (105m) is a short 1 km affair and warm-up for the Whangamoa (357m) & Rai Saddles (247m). The gradients are long, sometimes twisting but not excessively steep apart from 2 km sections each side of Rai Saddle. After Rai Village becomes flat with occasional undulations for 27 km to Havelock.

1 km after leaving Havelock take first left onto Queen Charlotte Drive. There follows 7 km of moderate hills along Pelorus Sound and several km of flat both side of Linkwater before returning to hills. The narrow winding road hugs the coast as it dips in and climbs out of tiny bays, goes round low headlands and ends with a final descent into Picton. Beware logging trucks between Nelson and Havelock.

ATTRACTIONS: Rai Village, Canvastown & Havelock dot the route from Nelson to Picton and are historic settlements established during a gold rush last century. Pass several scenic reserves notably Pelorus Bridge. Nearby is Marlborough Sounds Maritime Park with its maze of intricate bays & harbours. Many aquatic activities are available like boating, fishing, diving, sea-kayaking, mail boat run & guided tours. In recent years numerous mussel farms have sprung up throughout the sounds.

The sleepy fishing village of Havelock is the gateway to the sounds and boasts having Lord Rutherford as an ex-pupil of the old school. Pelorus & Queen Charlotte Sounds have tramping tracks offering fine views of picturesque bays. The Wellington ferry departs Picton.

OPTIONS: **ALTERNATIVE** NELSON - MAUNGATAPU SADDLE - PELORUS BRIDGE. 35km. For the adventurous! Much of the track is gravel, very rough and steep. Muddy when wet. A 500m climb in 4km to 720m followed by 600m descent in 7 km. No services. At Murderers' Rock 3 people were murdered in 1866, for the gold they carried. For lightly loaded bikes.

SIDE TRIP i RAI VALLEY VILLAGE - MARLBOROUGH SOUNDS Maritime Park along a hilly winding track to TENNYSON INLET and FRENCH PASS and many remote DoC camping areas. Havelock has only boat access to the park.

SIDE TRIP ii LINKWATER - PORTAGE - KENEPURU SOUND by road and deep into . . . MARLBOROUGH SOUNDS Maritime Park. Walk the Queen Charlotte Track in summer or ride it in winter. Small store at Waitaria Bay. Plenty of remote DoC camping areas. Hostel (bkpr at Hopewell, YHA at Kenepuru). Several lodges, farm & home stays in a various locations providing a variety of accommodation, check at Havelock or Picton before proceeding.

LINK ROAD HAVELOCK - BLENHEIM. Gradients fluctuate between flat and undulating passing OKARAMIO: (17 km) pub & RENWICK: (29 km) Supermarket, takeaways/tearooms, dairy, bkpr hostel, pub. A flat 10 km from Renwick, except a small hump, brings one to BLENHEIM see page 11.

IMPORTANT: NZ may be a pedallers' paradise but it isn't Utopia. So while preferring not to put off potential pedallers it is important to highlight possible hazards one could encounter.

TRAFFIC: Every country has its bad drivers and New Zealand is no exception. Only in the last few years have serious attempts been made to right some very bad habits, but it will probably take a long time to rectify. Drunk driving, travelling too fast and too close to the vehicle in front are the worst aspects.

If encountering dangerous drivers, try to get the vehicle's number and report it with relevant details, such as time and location, at the next police station. They can trace the vehicle and speak to the owner, it is better they act before someone is hurt. **A mirror is particularly useful**.

Try to be seen at all times. Cycling too close to the left may leave you too little room to manoeuvre. In cities, cycling too close to parked cars invites having a door open as you pass. Consider other road users, do not hold up traffic without good reason. Think of other cyclists who follow in your tyre tracks.

WIND: The wind can blow strong and hard. If it is so strong you have to pedal downhill to keep up momentum, then it is time to stop at the next location, or even turn round and go back. You're on holiday and this is supposed to be fun! Apart from the frustration of going nowhere fast it can be dangerous. There is less control of the bike and is often hard to hear traffic approaching from behind.

SANDFLIES: Apart from car drivers New Zealand has no dangerous animals such as bears or big pussy cats but certainly makes up for it with sandflies. Do not underestimate them!

MAGPIES: In spring during nesting season magpies use cyclists as target practice for dive bombing runs and have been known to draw blood! A suggestion is to draw two eyes on the back of the helmet, or your head. The theory is they only attack from behind. They're so unpopular, even Royal Forest & Bird Protection Society want them declared a pest. They seem to be worst on Canterbury back roads.

KEAS: You won't find any Norwegian Blues pining for the fiords (Monty Python types understand) but there is a mischievous native mountain parrot with a large sharp beak and curious nature. It's not into dive bombing but does steal things and has been known to rip expensive tent walls to get at tasty comestibles (food) rather than open the door. Found in all national parks with mountains and fiords!

SUN: Skin cancer is a problem in NZ due to the strength of the sun's ultra-violet rays penetrating the shrinking ozone layer. In summer use sun block on all exposed skin, forgetting to do so one day may cause severe sunburn, even when cloudy. Using a helmet with a peak or hat makes sense.

WATER: New Zealand was known as the only third world country where the water is safe to drink. While tap water is still fine, usually, care must be taken in the wilderness. It is recommended to boil drinking water because of the possible presence of the parasite giardia, a nasty bug that causes diarrhoea and stomach upsets. Even if giardia isn't present and sheep are, think twice about drinking from that cool sparkling crystal clear stream.

BIKE STANDS: The type found outside shops & libraries etc, where you put the front wheel. If using one with a fully laden bike then make sure the weight is balanced. Wheels have poor lateral strength and it could be banana shaped on your return!

TELEPHONES & CARDS: Coin phones outside cities are all but extinct. Rechargeable telephone cards offered by several companies are now available that are better value than the original rip-off Telecom throw away ones. Usually obtainable from hostels & motor camps.

SUMMER SCHOOL HOLIDAYS: Between 26th December and about 5th January many popular tourist locations fill up. These normally tiny communities swell to many thousands and finding even a tent space might be difficult.

TOURISM AWARDS: A company winning a toursim award may not always suggest a high level of customer satisfaction.

BACKPACKER BUSES: Actually their occupants. They have a reputation for making a lot of mess and noise late into the night at the places they stay. Just the thing after a long day in the saddle.

SOUTH ISLAND BICYCLE SHOPS (all telephone toll calls to these numbers have 03 prefix)

EAST

CHRISTCHURCH: *Cycle Trading Co, 27 Manchester St ☎366-3760.
*John Bull Cycles, Cnr Colombo & Lichfield St ☎377-2058.
*Papanui Cycles, 468 Papanui Rd ☎352-7495.
*Bicycle Business, 558 Colombo St ☎366-6466
*WheelsnDeals, 159 Gloucester St ☎377-6655.
*Pennys Cycles, Cnr Manchester/Tuam St ☎379-1520.
*Fleet Cycles, 280 Lincoln Road ☎338-9155.
*Cyclone Cycles, 245 Colombo St ☎332-9588 Not a complete list.
BLENHEIM: *Spokesman Cycles, 61 Queen St ☎578-0433.
*Reidie Redwood Village Cycles, 82 Cleghorn St ☎577-7202.
KAIKOURA: Kaikoura Sports, 21 West End ☎319-5370.
KAIAPOI: *Kaiapoi Cycles, 101 William St ☎327-8093.
RANGIORA: *Push Bikes, Gables Arcade ☎313-5298.
ASHBURTON: *Paul Wylie Cycles, 211 Burnett St ☎307-6443. *Arnst Cycle Centre, 90 Tancred St ☎308-2668.
TIMARU: *Cyclery, 106 Stafford St ☎688-8892. *Howes Cycles, 127 Church St ☎684-8900.
WAIMATE: Waimate Outdoors, 107 Queens St ☎689-7950.
OAMARU: *Martyn's Cycles, 51 Thames St ☎434-8416. *Victor Nelson, 231 Thames St ☎434-9077.
DUNEDIN: *Browns, Lower Stuart St ☎477-7259. *Cycle Surgery, 67 Stuart St ☎477-7473.
R & R Sport, 70 Stuart St, ☎474-1211.
MOSGIEL: *Sinclair Saws, 102 Gordon Rd ☎489-7777.
NASEBY: Royal Hotel, Earne St ☎444-9990??

CENTRAL

HANMER SPRINGS: Dust n Dirt, 20 Conical Hill, ☎315-7233.
REEFTON: Reefton Sports Centre, Broadway ☎732-8593.
GERALDINE: Flowerday Motorcycle Centre, Peel St ☎693-9107.
FAIRLIE: Brian Knight Motors, 83 Main Road ☎685-8301.
CROMWELL: Cycle Surgery, 48 The Mall ☎445-4100.
QUEENSTOWN: *Small Planet, Shotover St ☎442-6393. *The Bike Fix, The Mall ☎441-2299.
*Outside Sports, Camp St ☎442-8883.

SOUTH

QUEENSTOWN: See Central above.
TE ANAU: Fiordland Cycles, 197 Milford Rd ☎249-7460.
WINTON: Winton Mowers, 301 Great North Rd ☎236-8585.
INVERCARGILL: *Wensley's Cycles, Cnr Tay & Nith St ☎218-6206.
*Gladstones Cycles, 420 Dee St ☎218-8822. *Big on Bikes, 1 Dee St ☎214-4388.
GORE: *Outdoor Power, 189 Main St ☎208-7518. *Murray Kawasaki, Ordsal/Norfork Sts ☎208-6653.
MOSGIEL: *Sinclair Saws, 102 Gordon Rd ☎489-7777.
ALEXANDRA: *Cycle World, 21 Shannon St ☎448-8048. *Henderson Cycles, 88 Centenial Ave ☎448-8917.

WEST

WANAKA: *Jim & Libby's, 3 Helwick St ☎443-7259.
*Mountain Bikes Unlimited, Ardmore St ☎443-7882.
HOKITIKA: Hokitika Cycles, 33 Tancred St ☎755-8662.
GREYMOUTH: *Coll Sports World, 53 Mackay St ☎768-4060.
*Mann Cycles, 37 Mackay St ☎768-0255.
WESTPORT: *Beckers Cycles, 204 Palmerston St ☎789-8002.
*Gibson's Cycles, 180 Palmerston St ☎789-6293.

NORTH

RICHMOND: *Village Cycles, 301 Queens St ☎544-7166.
*Mall Cycles, Richmond Mall ☎544-8079.
STOKE: *Stoke Cycle Centre, 492 Main Rd ☎547-6361.
NELSON: *Natural High, 52 Rutherford St ☎546-6936.
*Stewart Cycles, 114 Hardy St ☎548-4344.
*Bridge St Cycles, 105 Bridge St ☎548-3877.
*Kelvin's Cycles, 109 Rutherford St ☎548-2851. Not a complete list.
MOTUEKA: Coppin's Outdoors Centre, 255 High St ☎528-7296.
TAKAKA: The Quiet Revolution Cycle Shop, 11 Commercial St ☎525-9555.

NOTE: Shops open, close or move. If possible, check for accuracy of the above before contacting

INDEX

UPDATES:

Visit **http://www.paradise-press.co.nz** for the latest updates, list of shops and other useful stuff. The **http://www.voyager.co.nz/~dabhand.html** is no longer active.

GENERAL: The following changes and errors have been found since going to print.

BIKE SHOPS: If possible try to check the address of bike shops if needing to contact them. Sometimes existing ones shut, move or new ones open.

PROFILES: The elevation scale on the profiles vary from graph to graph, which may be confusing for some users. In this reprint I've adjusted the profiles so the relationship to each other is better.

WATER: References to water at DoC camp sites or other such places does not imply it is suitable for drinking without proper treatment - even if it comes out of a tap!

Regretfully Pedallers' Paradise cyclists accommodation at Lake Tekapo has closed but we are trying to find a suitable place in Christchurch. There is more accommodation for cyclists on the previous page.